THE PELICAN SHAKESPEARE
GENERAL EDITOR : ALFRED HARBAGE
AB26
KING JOHN

WILLIAM SHAKESPEARE

The Life and Death of King John

EDITED BY IRVING RIBNER

PENGUIN BOOKS
BALTIMORE · MARYLAND

This edition first published 1962
Penguin Books Inc.
3300 Clipper Mill Road, Baltimore 11, Maryland

Printed in the United States of America

CONTENTS

SHAKESPEARE AND HIS STAGE

William Shakespeare was christened in Holy Trinity Church, Stratford-on-Avon, April 26, 1564. His birth is traditionally assigned to April 23rd. He was the eldest of four boys and two girls who survived infancy in the family of John Shakespeare, glover and trader of Henley Street, and his wife Mary Arden, daughter of a small landowner of Wilmcote. In 1568 John was elected Bailiff (equivalent to Mayor) of Stratford, having already filled the minor municipal offices. The town maintained for the sons of the burgesses a free school, taught by a university graduate and offering preparation in Latin sufficient for university entrance; its early registers are lost, but there can be little doubt that Shakespeare received the formal part of his education in this school.

On November 27, 1582, a license was issued for the marriage of William Shakespeare (aged eighteen) and Ann Hathaway (aged twenty-six), and on May 26, 1583, their child Susanna was christened in Holy Trinity Church. The inference that the marriage was forced upon the youth is natural but not inevitable; betrothal was legally binding at the time, and was sometimes regarded as conferring conjugal rights. Two additional children of the marriage, the twins Hamnet and Judith, were christened on February 2, 1585. Meanwhile the prosperity of the elder Shakespeares had declined, and William was impelled to seek a career outside Stratford.

The tradition that he spent some time as a country teacher is old but unverifiable. Because of the absence of records his

7

early twenties are called the "lost years," and only one thing about them is certain – that at least some of these years were spent in winning a place in the acting profession. He may have begun as a provincial trouper, but by 1592 he was established in London and prominent enough to be attacked. In a pamphlet of that year, *Groatsworth of Wit*, the ailing Robert Greene complained of the neglect which university writers like himself had suffered from actors, one of whom was daring to set up as a playwright:

> ... an upstart crow beautified with our feathers, that with his *Tiger's heart wrapt in a player's hide* supposes he is as well able to bombast out a blank verse as the best of you, and being an absolute Johannes-factotum, is in his own conceit the only Shake-scene in a country.

The pun on his name, and the parody of his line "O tiger's heart wrapt in a woman's hide" (*III Henry VI*), pointed clearly to Shakespeare. Some of his admirers protested, and Henry Chettle, the editor of Greene's pamphlet, saw fit to apologize:

> I am as sorry as if the original fault had been my fault, because myself have seen his demeanor no less civil than he excellent in the quality he professes. Besides divers of worship have reported his uprightness of dealing, which argues his honesty, and his facetious grace in writing that approves his art. (Prefatory epistle, *Kind Heart's Dream*)

The plague closed the London theatres for many months in 1593–94, denying the actors their livelihood. To this period belong Shakespeare's two narrative poems, *Venus and Adonis* and *Rape of Lucrece*, both dedicated to the Earl

8

of Southampton. No doubt the poet was rewarded with a gift of money as usual in such cases, but he did no further dedicating and we have no reliable information on whether Southampton, or anyone else, became his regular patron. His sonnets, first mentioned in 1598 and published without his consent in 1609, are intimate without being explicitly autobiographical. They seem to commemorate the poet's friendship with an idealized youth, rivalry with a more favored poet, and love affair with a dark mistress; and his bitterness when the mistress betrays him in conjunction with the friend; but it is difficult to decide precisely what the "story" is, impossible to decide whether it is fictional or true. The real distinction of the sonnets, at least of those not purely conventional, rests in the universality of the thoughts and moods they express, and in their poignancy and beauty.

In 1594 was formed the theatrical company known until 1603 as the Lord Chamberlain's Men, thereafter as the King's Men. Its original membership included, besides Shakespeare, the beloved clown Will Kempe and the famous actor Richard Burbage. The company acted in various London theatres and even toured the provinces, but it is chiefly associated in our minds with the Globe Theatre built on the south bank of the Thames in 1599. Shakespeare was an actor and joint owner of this company (and its Globe) through the remainder of his creative years. His plays, written at the average rate of two a year, together with Burbage's acting won it its place of leadership among the London companies.

Individual plays began to appear in print, in editions both honest and piratical, and the publishers became increasingly aware of the value of Shakespeare's name on the title pages. As early as 1598 he was hailed as the leading English dramatist in the *Palladis Tamia* of Francis Meres:

As Plautus and Seneca are accounted the best for Comedy and Tragedy among the Latins, so Shakespeare among the English is the most excellent in both kinds for the stage: for Comedy, witness his *Gentlemen of Verona*, his *Errors*, his *Love labors lost*, his *Love labors won* [*Taming of the Shrew?*], his *Midsummers night dream*, & his *Merchant of Venice;* for Tragedy, his *Richard the 2*, *Richard the 3*, *Henry the 4*, *King John*, *Titus Andronicus*, and his *Romeo and Juliet*.

The note is valuable, both in indicating Shakespeare's prestige and in helping us to establish a chronology. In the second half of his writing career, history plays gave place to the great tragedies; and farces and light comedies gave place to the problem plays and symbolic romances. In 1623, seven years after his death, his former fellow actors, John Hemming and Henry Condell, cooperated with a group of London printers in bringing out his plays in collected form. The volume is generally known as the First Folio.

Shakespeare had never severed his relations with Stratford. His wife and children may sometimes have shared his London lodgings, but their home was Stratford. His son Hamnet was buried there in 1596, and his daughters Susanna and Judith were married there in 1607 and 1616 respectively. (His father, for whom he had secured a coat of arms and thus the privilege of writing himself gentleman, died in 1601, his mother in 1608.) His considerable earnings in London, as actor-sharer, part owner of the Globe, and playwright, were invested chiefly in Stratford property. In 1597 he purchased for £60 New Place, one of the two most imposing residences in the town. A number of other business transactions, as well as minor episodes in his career, have left documentary records. By 1611 he was in a position to retire, and he seems gradually to have withdrawn from theatrical activity in order to live in Stratford. In March, 1616, he made a will, leaving token bequests to Burbage, Hemming, and Condell, but the bulk of his estate to his family. The most famous feature of the will, the bequest of the second-best bed to his wife, reveals nothing about Shakespeare's marriage; the quaintness of the provision seems commonplace to those familiar with ancient testaments. Shakespeare died April 23, 1616, and was buried in the Stratford church where he had been christened. Within seven years a monument was erected to his memory on the north wall of the chancel. Its portrait bust and the Droeshout engraving on the title page of the First Folio provide the only likenesses with an established claim to authenticity. The best verbal vignette was written by his rival Ben Jonson, the more impressive for being imbedded in a context mainly critical:

> ... I loved the man, and do honor his memory (on this side idolatry) as much as any. He was indeed honest, and of an open and free nature: he had an excellent fancy, brave notions, and gentle expressions. ... (*Timber or Discoveries*, c. 1623-30)

The reader of Shakespeare's plays is aided by a general knowledge of the way in which they were staged. The King's Men acquired a roofed and artificially lighted theatre only toward the close of Shakespeare's career, and then only for winter use. Nearly all his plays were designed for performance in such structures as the Globe — a three-tiered amphitheatre with a large rectangular platform extending to the center of its yard. The plays were staged by daylight, by large casts brilliantly costumed, but with only a minimum of properties, without scenery, and quite possibly without intermissions. There was a rear stage balcony for action "above," and a curtained rear recess for "discoveries" and other special effects, but by far the major portion of any play was enacted upon the projecting platform, with episode following episode in swift succession, and with shifts of time and place signaled the audience only by the momentary clearing of the stage between the episodes. Information about the identity of the characters and, when necessary, about the time and place of the action was incorporated in the dialogue. No additional indications of place have been inserted in the present editions; these are apt to obscure the original fluidity of structure, with the emphasis upon action and speech rather than scenic background. The acting, including that of the youthful apprentices to the profession who performed the parts of women, was highly skillful, with a premium placed upon grace of gesture and beauty of diction. The audiences, a cross section of the general public, commonly numbered a thousand, sometimes more than two thousand. Judged by the type of plays they applauded, these audiences were not only large but also perceptive.

THE TEXTS OF THE PLAYS

About half of Shakespeare's plays appeared in print for the first time in the folio volume of 1623. The others had been published individually, usually in quarto volumes, during his lifetime or in the six years following his death. The copy used by the printers of the quartos varied greatly in merit, sometimes representing Shakespeare's true text, sometimes only a debased version of that text. The copy used by the printers of the folio also varied in merit, but was chosen with care. Since it consisted of the best available manuscripts, or the more acceptable quartos (although frequently in editions other than the first), or of quartos corrected by reference to manuscripts, we have good or reasonably good texts of most of the thirty-seven plays.

In the present series, the plays have been newly edited from quarto or folio texts depending, when a choice offered, upon which is now regarded by bibliographical specialists as the more authoritative. The ideal has been to reproduce the chosen texts with as few alterations as possible, beyond occasional relineation, expansion of abbreviations, and modernization of punctuation and spelling. Emendation is held to a minimum, and such material as has been added, in the way of stage directions and lines supplied by an alternative text, has been enclosed in square brackets.

None of the plays printed in Shakespeare's lifetime were divided into acts and scenes, and the inference is that the author's own manuscripts were not so divided. In the folio collection, some of the plays remained undivided, some were divided into acts, and some were divided into acts and scenes. During the eighteenth century all of the plays were divided into acts and scenes, and in the Cambridge edition of the mid-nineteenth century, from which the influential Globe text derived, this division was more or less regularized and the lines were numbered. Many useful works of reference employ the act-scene-line apparatus established by the Globe text.

Since the act-scene division thus established is obviously convenient, but is of very dubious authority so far as Shakespeare's own structural principles are concerned, or the original manner of staging his plays, a problem is presented to modern editors. In the present series the act-scene division of the Globe text is retained marginally, and may be viewed as a reference aid like the line numbering. A printer's ornament marks the points of division when these points have been determined by a cleared stage indicating a shift of time and place in the action of the play, or when no harm results from the editorial assumption that there is such a shift. However, at those points where the established division is clearly misleading – that is, where continuous action has been split up into separate "scenes" – the ornament is omitted and the distortion corrected. This mechanical expedient seemed the best means of combining utility and accuracy.

The General Editor.

INTRODUCTION

King John is not only a powerful and moving drama in its
own right, but it is particularly interesting for the insight it
affords into Shakespeare's development as a dramatic artist,
since it occupies a pivotal position in relation to his history
plays as well as his tragedies. As a history play, it reveals
Shakespeare's mastery of techniques he had employed in the
looser, more episodic *Henry VI* plays and *Richard III,* and
his experimentation with techniques he was to master in
Richard II and the *Henry IV* plays. As a tragedy, it is interesting for its conception of a hero frustrated by a sin which he
repents but cannot cancel, doomed to destruction by his
commitment to evil means in striving for great ends. With
such a view of man Shakespeare had dealt in the earlier
Titus Andronicus, and he was to return to it with greater
power in such plays as *Julius Caesar* and *Coriolanus.* As
Shakespeare's revision of *The Troublesome Reign of John,* an
anonymous two-part play printed in 1591, *King John* ena-
bles us to see how Shakespeare could shape the crude matter
of an unpalatable source play into a sophisticated and original work of art.

History and tragedy are closely fused in *King John,* for the
hero is destroyed by complicity in the death of Arthur, son
of his elder brother Geoffrey, and thus with a better claim
to the throne than his own. The king's sin is dictated by
political necessity, for Arthur's claim can lead only to per-
petual civil war; and Arthur stands, moreover, for the
power of Rome, supported by France and Austria. The
opposing political forces are clearly aligned at the beginning

15

of the play: John and the Bastard stand for English nationalism and royal supremacy, while Arthur stands for a divided
England, prey to invading foreign forces and subject to the
power of the papacy. John represents principles dear to
Tudor Englishmen, and his cause must triumph, but Shakespeare, in his usual manner, tempers the emotional commitment of his audience to the Tudor political position by his
portrait of the cruel Queen Elinor and by causing this position to demand the death of a child, as he similarly heightens
sympathy for Arthur by his portrait of the pathetic Constance. The tragedy of King John is that to attain political
victory he must sacrifice his own humanity. He is destroyed
by a cleavage between his public and private morality, just
as a similar division in a somewhat later play is to destroy
the noble Brutus of *Julius Caesar*.

Unfortunately there is no external evidence of any kind
as to the date of *King John,* but its stylistic relation to the
plays which clearly preceded it and to those which seem to
have followed it would suggest that it was written some-
time between 1592 and 1596, with 1594 perhaps most likely.
It follows *The Troublesome Reign* closely, although it tempers the virulent anti-Catholicism of the source, omitting
the most offensive scenes, perhaps – as has been suggested–
out of deference to the Catholic Earl of Southampton whose
patronage Shakespeare was seeking. It has been suggested in
recent years that the play may have been written as early as
1590, based directly on Holinshed's *Chronicles,* Foxe's *Book
of Martyrs,* the *Historia Maior* of Matthew Paris, and several
Latin chronicles which could have been available to Shakespeare only in manuscript. This theory would hold further
that *The Troublesome Reign,* printed in 1591, is not Shakespeare's source, but rather a corrupt version (bad quarto) of a
play written in imitation of Shakespeare's some months later

in the same year of 1590. Were this theory sustained, we would have to reconsider many of our views of *King John*, but it has won little acceptance among scholars, since it is based upon very tenuous "evidence" involving hypotheses more difficult to entertain than the simpler one that *The Troublesome Reign* was the earlier of the two plays and Shakespeare's source.

King John would have been "timely" whatever its date, since it deals with political issues which had come to be associated by Tudor historians with the reign of its titular character; we must remember that a very important value of history in Shakespeare's day was its power to teach political lessons, and that Shakespeare was, to some extent, bound in this play by the view of King John which had been shaped before him by Protestant chroniclers and by the political issues which they had found inherent in his story. We must note that a central issue of the play (as of its source) – the relation of England to the church of Rome—was also the most pressing political problem of Shakespeare's England, and that many Elizabethan writers were particularly interested in King John because they saw his reign as parallel in many respects to that of their own queen.

Although the early British historians, right through the Romanist Polydore Vergil, had been fairly harsh in their treatment of King John, with the Reformation we note a change. William Tyndale in 1528 accused the chronicles of distortion and praised John for his opposition to the papacy. Tyndale was followed in this by John Bale, a fiery Reformation polemicist, who in the following decade wrote a two-part morality play called *Kynge Johan* in which he used John's career to champion the cause of the Reformation. King John was similarly eulogized by the reformer John Foxe in his *Book of Martyrs,* and this Protestant view was adopted by chroniclers such as Richard Grafton and Raphael Holinshed, upon whose works *The Troublesome Reign* was based; and they were works Shakespeare undoubtedly read also before revising the old play. These writers, with little regard for historical fact, had made King John into a pre-Reformation hero, a king before Henry VIII who had dared oppose the papacy. He was not the tyrannical signer of *Magna Carta* whom we know. Indeed, *Magna Carta* receives no mention in this play, for it was regarded by Shakespeare's contemporaries not as a triumph for liberty, but rather as a shameful attempt to weaken the central monarchy in which most Elizabethans firmly believed, and whose virtues they saw reflected in the absolute rule of Queen Elizabeth. John to them was rather the symbol of English nationalism who had rallied the dissident barons against France and Austria, as well as the champion of royal supremacy who had defied the papal legate and died a martyr, poisoned by a treacherous monk, although historically King John appears to have died of overeating.

Shakespeare's play is informed by this view of King John, and like its source it asserts the doctrines which John's career commonly was called upon to illustrate: nationalism, royal supremacy, the evils of rebellion, and the right of a king to be answerable for his sins to God alone. But more than anything else – and here Shakespeare goes beyond his sources and reveals his own particular bent – the play affirms the inseparability of public and private virtue, that only a good man can be a good king. It asserts also that a nation can be united only when a king has learned to subordinate his personal desires to the good of his country. These themes are carried in the parallel progressions of King John and the Bastard, Faulconbridge, two characters created as foils to one another, the Bastard strong where John is weak and learning to rise and re-establish the glory of England as John declines and lets it fall. By their relation to one another the play is unified. When the Bastard surrenders his power to the new king in the final act, the audience sees that the goal of national unity which John had vainly sought has in fact been realized. John the man has been destroyed, but England, through the Bastard, is nevertheless triumphant.

Shakespeare makes clear that John is a usurper, but he establishes also that until the death of Arthur, John is a good, even a great, king, and that as the *de facto* ruler he merits the support of the nobility, a political point to be made again in the *Henry IV* plays. Arthur's inadequacy is emphasized by his own weakness and by the forces with whom he is associated. He stands also for the kind of child king which Tudor Englishmen conventionally mirrored in the unfortunate Henry VI, and such as they feared most among the possible successors to the now old and ailing Queen Elizabeth. John's greatness appears in his defiance of the French ambassador and the papal legate, in his victory before Angiers, and in the love and loyalty with which he is served by Faulconbridge, one of the most remarkable creations of Shakespeare's early career, a character so dear to audiences that some critics have been tempted to see him as the hero of the play, although to do so is to distort *King John* and destroy its unity.

John is the hero, and his greatness is emphasized up to the middle of the third act. He begins to degenerate both as man and as king when in III, iii he calls for the murder of Arthur. The Bastard, conversely, wins little triumph until the beginning of John's decline. At the beginning of the play he is fairly low on Fortune's wheel, a landless bastard, albeit the son of Coeur-de-lion, bearing the moral stigma of his illegitimacy, which he affirms proudly in spite of his mother's shame. He has a straightforward heartiness and charm which immediately win us to him, but he has little initial claim to virtue. Only as John declines does the Bastard's moral stature begin to be evident, becoming more and more clear until he is ready to assume the leadership of England which John, because of his own sin, can no longer bear.

The role of Constance is relatively brief, but historically it has been prized by actresses and has been performed by some of the greatest, although her savage interchange with Queen Elinor usually has been omitted on the stage. She is the last of Shakespeare's wailing women, bridging the gap between the weeping queens of *Richard III* and the queen of *Richard II,* with her gentle, more controlled, and finally more moving sorrow. The lamentations of Constance may disturb modern audiences by their excess, but they are Shakespeare's dramatic means of swaying the sympathies of his audience away from King John in the third act, and when this has been accomplished Constance drops out of the play. The alienation of the audience from John is completed in the scene, almost too painful to be staged, in which Arthur pleads with Hubert for his eyes. We now behold the fall of John and the collapse of his power as Hubert shows his inability to execute his commission and as England's enemies prepare their forces for a new onslaught. The fourth act shows us not a triumphant King John but a fearful one, vainly trusting in a new coronation to consolidate the power which the audience knows he has lost already. He is now struck repeated blows: he learns that his mother is dead, that his nobles have deserted him, and that the French army is prepared to invade England. He sees at once that his troubles all stem from his order to Hubert. He is torn by remorse – there is no pretense in his joy when he hears that

Arthur has not been killed after all — but his remorse is of no avail, and even though he has had no hand in the actual death of Arthur he must bear the guilt for it. How abject and powerless he has now become appears in his ignominious capitulation to the papal legate he had once so proudly defied.

When the Bastard castigates Hubert for the death of Arthur, Shakespeare is placing Faulconbridge in opposition to what John has become, aligning him clearly on the side of virtue. He has every reason to desert John, but in spite of Arthur's death he decides to remain with his king rather than join the rebelling nobles, and in this decision he attains his full stature, for he masters his own personal passion and places the good of England above all other considerations. He now becomes the symbol of English strength and unity, and it is only fitting that John should relinquish his power to him. Before this symbol the French army is powerless; John's capitulation to Pandulph is undone, the rebellious lords are won back to the crown, and the Bastard closes the play with his great apostrophe to England. He might at the end become king himself, but he recognizes the primacy of legitimate succession, and in surrendering his power to the young Henry III he sets the welfare of England above his personal glory, assuring to his country a continuance of orderly government, with a lawful king upon the throne. Under the new regime England will enjoy a greater degree of felicity than it had ever known under King John, and in assuring this the triumph of Faulconbridge is both an ethical and a political one, for while serving his country he has learned also to master himself.

In Shakespeare's English history plays the kingdom itself is conceived of as a kind of dramatic entity, for in its welfare dramatic interest is always centered. In this play England is finally victorious in spite of the sins of her king, and she is able to achieve victory through the rise of Faulconbridge, who comes to occupy John's forfeited role and to stand for the political and ethical ideals which John was incapable of attaining. The king himself dies ignobly, but Shakespeare suggests (V, vii, 70–73) that he is able at last to save his soul. His sincere remorse for the death of Arthur, and the victory of England in spite of all, win for him the possibility of expiation. Faulconbridge and Prince Henry indicate Shakespeare's final judgment as they sing the dead king's praises. King John dies not a treacherous villain but the royal martyr he had been made into before Shakespeare approached the subject.

Although there is no evidence of a specific performance of *King John* earlier than the revival at Covent Garden by John Rich in 1737, the play has been fairly popular ever since. In early performances the part of Arthur was played usually by a girl, and even more unfortunate, during the eighteenth and nineteenth centuries the play was often adapted and distorted for purposes of political propaganda, the most notable instance being Colley Cibber's *Papal Tyranny in the Reign of King John,* produced at Covent Garden in 1745, after many years of preparation, with Cibber making his final stage appearance as Pandulph. Five days after this opening David Garrick launched a rival version – presumably going back to Shakespeare – at Drury Lane, playing the part of John himself. In later years he played the Bastard as well, but he always preferred the titular role. The play had its first American production in Philadelphia in 1768.

King John owes much of its stage popularity to the appeal for actors of three great roles: King John, the Bastard, and Constance. These parts have been played by the greatest figures in both the British and American theater. The play was a favorite in the repertory of John Philip Kemble and Sarah Siddons from 1783 until their retirement, Mrs. Siddons playing Constance for the last time in 1812 and Kemble appearing as John just a few days before he left the stage in 1817. Edmund and Charles Kean, William Macready, and Sir Herbert Beerbohm Tree were all responsible for memorable productions, as were Edwin Booth and Robert Mantell in the United States. In more recent years the play has had a new burst of popularity, and scarcely a year goes by without at least one important production. *King John* has all the ingredients of great drama: action, character, poetry, and a presiding moral vision.

Tulane University   IRVING RIBNER

Note on the text: This edition follows closely the only substantive text of *King John,* that of the first folio (1623). The folio text seems to have been set up from Shakespeare's own draft, possibly corrected before printing, particularly in the two final acts, by reference to the theatre prompt copy. It is a fairly good text, but it shows some confusion and inconsistency in the names of characters in speech headings and stage directions. These have been corrected and regularized in the present edition, and a few additional emendations have been made, as listed below. The folio text is divided, somewhat haphazardly, into acts and scenes. The act-scene division here supplied marginally is that of the Globe text, with an adjustment at III, iii indicated in the manner described in the general introduction.

The following substantive departures (in italic type) have been made from the folio text. Some are readings from the second (1632), third (1663), or fourth (1683) folios; others are emendations made early in the history of Shakespearean scholarship and accepted by most modern editors. The authority for each is indicated parenthetically, followed by the first folio reading (in roman type).

I, i, 147 *I would* (F2) It would   237 *Could he get me* (Vaughan) Could get me   257 *Thou art* (F4) That art

II, i, 1 *King Philip* (Theobald) Lewis   63 *Ate* (Rowe) Ace   113 *breast* (F2) beast   144 *shows* (Theobald) shooes   149 *King Philip* (Theobald) King Lewis   150 *King Philip* (Theobald) Lewis   215 *Confront* (Rowe)

Comfort 259 *roundure* (Capell) rounder 325 *Citizen* (Rowe) Hubert
335 *run* (F2) room 368 *Citizen* (Rowe) Fra. 371 *Kinged* (Tyrwhitt)
Kings 416 *Citizen* (Rowe) Hubert

III, i, 110 *day* (Theobald) daies 148 *task* (Theobald) tast

III, iii, 39 *ear* (Collier) race

III, iv, 44 *not holy* (F4) holy 64 *friends* (Rowe) fiends 110 *world's*
(Pope) words

IV, i, 92 *mote* (Wilson) moth

IV, ii, 1 *again* (F3) against 42 *when* (Tyrwhitt) then 73 *Does* (F4) Do

IV, iii, 33 *man* (F2) mans 41 *Have you* (F3) you have 155 *ceinture*
(Moore Smith) center

V, ii, 26 *Were* (F2) Was 36 *grapple* (Pope) cripple 43 *hast thou* (F4)
hast 135 *these* (Rowe) this

V, vi, 12 *eyeless* (Theobald) endless

V, vii, 17 *mind* (Rowe) winde 21 *cygnet* (Rowe) Symet 42 *strait* (Pope)
straight 108 *give you thanks* (Rowe) giue thankes

24

The Life and Death
of King John

THE LIFE AND DEATH
OF KING JOHN

Enter King John, Queen Elinor, Pembroke, Essex, and
   Salisbury, with the Chatillion of France.

King John. Now, say, Chatillion, what would France with us?
Chatillion. Thus, after greeting, speaks the King of France
  In my behavior to the majesty,
  The borrowed majesty, of England here.
Elinor. A strange beginning: 'borrowed majesty'!   5
King John. Silence, good mother; hear the embassy.
Chatillion. Philip of France, in right and true behalf
  Of thy deceasèd brother Geoffrey's son,
  Arthur Plantagenet, lays most lawful claim
  To this fair island and the territories,   10
  To Ireland, Poitiers, Anjou, Touraine, Maine,
  Desiring thee to lay aside the sword
  Which sways usurpingly these several titles,
  And put the same into young Arthur's hand,
  Thy nephew and right royal sovereign.   15

I, i, 3 *In my behavior* through my person   4 *borrowed* stolen   6 *embassy*
message   7 *in right and true behalf* in support of the lawful claim

27

King John. What follows if we disallow of this?

Chatillion. The proud control of fierce and bloody war,
To enforce these rights so forcibly withheld.

King John. Here have we war for war and blood for blood,
20 Controlment for controlment; so answer France.

Chatillion. Then take my king's defiance from my mouth,
The farthest limit of my embassy.

King John. Bear mine to him, and so depart in peace.
Be thou as lightning in the eyes of France,
25 For, ere thou canst report, I will be there.
The thunder of my cannon shall be heard.
So, hence! Be thou the trumpet of our wrath
And sullen presage of your own decay.
An honorable conduct let him have;
30 Pembroke, look to 't. Farewell, Chatillion.

                                        Exit Chatillion and Pembroke.

Elinor. What now, my son! Have I not ever said
How that ambitious Constance would not cease
Till she had kindled France and all the world
Upon the right and party of her son?
35 This might have been prevented and made whole
With very easy arguments of love,
Which now the manage of two kingdoms must
With fearful bloody issue arbitrate.

King John. Our strong possession and our right for us.

Elinor. Your strong possession much more than your
40   right,
Or else it must go wrong with you and me —

16 *disallow of* refuse 17 *proud control* overbearing compulsion 20 *Controlment* compulsion 25 *report* deliver your message (with secondary meaning of thunder) 26 *cannon* (an anachronism, since gunpowder had not yet been invented) 27 *trumpet* (as a herald) 28 *decay* destruction 29 *conduct* escort 36 *arguments of love* (1) expressions of affection (2) friendly discussions 37 *manage* government

So much my conscience whispers in your ear,
Which none but heaven, and you, and I, shall hear.

Enter a Sheriff [who speaks aside to Essex].

Essex. My liege, here is the strangest controversy,
Come from the country to be judged by you,   45
That e'er I heard. Shall I produce the men?
King John. Let them approach.
Our abbeys and our priories shall pay
This expeditious charge.

*Enter Robert Faulconbridge, and Philip [his bastard
brother].*

                            What men are you?
Bastard. Your faithful subject, I, a gentleman,   50
Born in Northamptonshire, and eldest son,
As I suppose, to Robert Faulconbridge,
A soldier, by the honor-giving hand
Of Cordelion knighted in the field.
King John. What art thou?   55
Robert. The son and heir to that same Faulconbridge.
King John. Is that the elder, and art thou the heir?
You came not of one mother then, it seems.
Bastard. Most certain of one mother, mighty king;
That is well known; and, as I think, one father.   60
But for the certain knowledge of that truth
I put you o'er to heaven and to my mother.
Of that I doubt, as all men's children may.
Elinor. Out on thee, rude man! Thou dost shame thy
    mother
And wound her honor with this diffidence.   65

49 *expeditious* speedy, sudden 54 *Cordelion* Coeur-de-lion, i.e. King
Richard I 62 *put you o'er* refer you 65 *diffidence* distrust

29

Bastard. I, madam? No, I have no reason for it;
    That is my brother's plea and none of mine;
    The which if he can prove, 'a pops me out
    At least from fair five hundred pound a year.
70   Heaven guard my mother's honor and my land!
King John. A good blunt fellow. Why, being younger born,
    Doth he lay claim to thine inheritance?
Bastard. I know not why, except to get the land.
    But once he slandered me with bastardy.
75   But whe'r I be as true begot or no,
    That still I lay upon my mother's head;
    But that I am as well begot, my liege –
    Fair fall the bones that took the pains for me –
    Compare our faces and be judge yourself.
80   If old Sir Robert did beget us both,
    And were our father, and this son like him,
    O old Sir Robert, father, on my knee
    I give heaven thanks I was not like to thee!
King John. Why, what a madcap hath heaven lent us here!
85 *Elinor.* He hath a trick of Cordelion's face;
    The accent of his tongue affecteth him.
    Do you not read some tokens of my son
    In the large composition of this man?
King John. Mine eye hath well examinèd his parts,
90   And finds them perfect Richard. Sirrah, speak.
    What doth move you to claim your brother's land?
Bastard. Because he hath a half-face like my father.
    With half that face would he have all my land –
    A half-faced groat five hundred pound a year!

68 *'a* he   74 *once* on a single occasion which he dare not repeat   75 *whe'r*
whether   76 *lay . . . head* let my mother account for   78 *fall* befall   85 *trick*
characteristic expression   86 *affecteth* resembles   92 *half-face* profile (with
secondary meaning of imperfect)   94 *half-faced groat* a thin silver coin
with a profile stamped upon it, also an imperfect or inferior coin

Robert. My gracious liege, when that my father lived,   95
  Your brother did employ my father much —
Bastard. Well, sir, by this you cannot get my land.
  Your tale must be how he employed my mother.
Robert. And once dispatched him in an embassy
  To Germany, there with the emperor   100
  To treat of high affairs touching that time.
  Th' advantage of his absence took the king,
  And in the mean time sojourned at my father's;
  Where how he did prevail I shame to speak,
  But truth is truth; large lengths of seas and shores   105
  Between my father and my mother lay,
  As I have heard my father speak himself,
  When this same lusty gentleman was got.
  Upon his death-bed he by will bequeathed
  His lands to me, and took it on his death   110
  That this my mother's son was none of his;
  And if he were, he came into the world
  Full fourteen weeks before the course of time.
  Then, good my liege, let me have what is mine,
  My father's land, as was my father's will.   115
King John. Sirrah, your brother is legitimate.
  Your father's wife did after wedlock bear him,
  And if she did play false, the fault was hers,
  Which fault lies on the hazards of all husbands
  That marry wives. Tell me, how if my brother,   120
  Who, as you say, took pains to get this son,
  Had of your father claimed this son for his?
  In sooth, good friend, your father might have kept
  This calf, bred from his cow, from all the world.

99 *dispatched* sent   104 *shame* am ashamed   108 *lusty* merry   *got* conceived   110 *took it on his death* swore on his deathbed (the most solemn kind of oath)   119 *lies on the hazards* is one of the risks

125   In sooth he might; then, if he were my brother's,
      My brother might not claim him, nor your father,
      Being none of his, refuse him. This concludes;
      My mother's son did get your father's heir;
      Your father's heir must have your father's land.
130 *Robert.* Shall then my father's will be of no force
      To dispossess that child which is not his?
     Bastard. Of no more force to dispossess me, sir,
      Than was his will to get me, as I think.
     Elinor. Whether hadst thou rather be a Faulconbridge,
135   And like thy brother, to enjoy thy land,
      Or the reputed son of Cordelion,
      Lord of thy presence and no land beside?
     Bastard. Madam, and if my brother had my shape
      And I had his, Sir Robert's his, like him,
140   And if my legs were two such riding-rods,
      My arms such eel-skins stuffed, my face so thin
      That in mine ear I durst not stick a rose
      Lest men should say, 'Look, where three-farthings goes!'
      And, to his shape, were heir to all this land,
145   Would I might never stir from off this place,
      I would give it every foot to have this face;
      I would not be Sir Nob in any case.
     Elinor. I like thee well. Wilt thou forsake thy fortune,
      Bequeath thy land to him, and follow me?
150   I am a soldier and now bound to France.
     Bastard. Brother, take you my land, I'll take my chance.

127 *refuse* disclaim *concludes* settles the question decisively 135 *like thy brother* i.e. in physical appearance (being of the same father), and therefore not a bastard, entitled to his land 137 *presence* person 140 *riding-rods* switches used by riders 142–43 *ear…goes* (certain coins were distinguished from others by a rose behind Queen Elizabeth's head; he is saying that his brother dare not place a rose behind his ear, as a lover might, lest he be taken for a three-farthing piece, his face being so thin)

Your face hath got five hundred pound a year,
Yet sell your face for five pence and 'tis dear.
Madam, I'll follow you unto the death.

Elinor. Nay, I would have you go before me thither.   155

Bastard. Our country manners give our betters way.

King John. What is thy name?

Bastard. Philip, my liege, so is my name begun;
Philip, good old Sir Robert's wife's eldest son.

King John. From henceforth bear his name whose form
thou bearest.   160
Kneel thou down Philip, but rise more great;
Arise Sir Richard, and Plantagenet.

Bastard. Brother by th' mother's side, give me your hand.
My father gave me honor, yours gave land.
Now blessèd be the hour, by night or day,   165
When I was got, Sir Robert was away!

Elinor. The very spirit of Plantagenet!
I am thy grandam, Richard; call me so.

Bastard. Madam, by chance but not by truth; what though?
Something about, a little from the right,   170
In at the window, or else o'er the hatch:
Who dares not stir by day must walk by night,
And have is have, however men do catch.
Near or far off, well won is still well shot,
And I am I, howe'er I was begot.   175

King John. Go, Faulconbridge. Now hast thou thy desire;
A landless knight makes thee a landed squire.
Come, madam, and come, Richard, we must speed
For France, for France, for it is more than need.

160 *form* physical characteristics 165 *hour* (with a possible pun on 'whore,'
since both words were pronounced identically) 169 *truth* honesty, chaste
conduct 171 *In . . . hatch* (proverbial expressions referring to illegitimate
birth) 177 *landless knight* i.e. the Bastard (who has just renounced his
land in favor of his brother)

180 *Bastard.* Brother, adieu; good fortune come to thee!
     For thou wast got i' th' way of honesty.
                                              Exeunt all but Bastard.

     A foot of honor better than I was,
     But many a many foot of land the worse.
     Well, now can I make any Joan a lady.
185 'Good den, Sir Richard!' – 'God-a-mercy, fellow' –
     And if his name be George, I'll call him Peter,
     For new-made honor doth forget men's names;
     'Tis too respective and too sociable
     For your conversion. Now your traveller,
190 He and his toothpick at my worship's mess,
     And when my knightly stomach is sufficed,
     Why then I suck my teeth and catechize
     My pickèd man of countries: 'My dear sir' –
     Thus, leaning on mine elbow, I begin –
195 'I shall beseech you' – that is question now;
     And then comes answer like an Absey-book;
     'O, sir,' says answer, 'at your best command,
     At your employment, at your service, sir';
     'No, sir,' says question, 'I, sweet sir, at yours';
200 And so, ere answer knows what question would,
     Saving in dialogue of compliment,
     And talking of the Alps and Apennines,
     The Pyrenean and the river Po,
     It draws toward supper in conclusion so.

184 *Joan* (name used for any girl of lowly station) 185 *Good den* God give
you good even   *God-a-mercy* God reward you   188 *respective* respectful,
courteous   189 *conversion* change of status   190 *toothpick* (a sign of affectation, associated particularly with the foreign traveller)   *mess* dinner
table   193 *pickèd* (1) refined, rarefied (2) whose teeth have been picked
196 *Absey-book* ABC book, primer for instruction of children (the Bastard
is mimicking the kind of question-and-answer exercise found in such
books)   201 *dialogue of compliment* formal, elegant address

But this is worshipful society,   205
And fits the mounting spirit like myself,
For he is but a bastard to the time
That doth not smack of observation.
And so am I, whether I smack or no,
And not alone in habit and device,   210
Exterior form, outward accoutrement,
But from the inward motion to deliver
Sweet, sweet, sweet poison for the age's tooth,
Which, though I will not practise to deceive,
Yet, to avoid deceit, I mean to learn;   215
For it shall strew the footsteps of my rising.
But who comes in such haste in riding-robes?
What woman-post is this? Hath she no husband
That will take pains to blow a horn before her?

Enter Lady Faulconbridge and James Gurney.

O me! 'Tis my mother. How now, good lady!   220
What brings you here to court so hastily?
Lady Faulconbridge. Where is that slave, thy brother?
    Where is he,
That holds in chase mine honor up and down?
Bastard. My brother Robert? Old Sir Robert's son?
    Colbrand the giant, that same mighty man?   225
Is it Sir Robert's son that you seek so?
Lady Faulconbridge. Sir Robert's son! Ay, thou unreverend
    boy,

---

207 *bastard to the time* no true son of the age 208 *observation* obsequiousness
210 *habit* dress 212 *motion* impulse 213 *Sweet . . . poison* flattery
215 *deceit* being deceived 216 *it . . . rising* i.e. flattery will ac-
company his rise to greatness as rushes are strewn upon a great man's floor
218 *woman-post* female courier 219 *blow a horn* i.e. announce his cuck-
oldry and her infidelity 223 *holds in chase* pursues to destroy 225 *Col-
brand* a Danish giant killed by Guy of Warwick in the old romance

Sir Robert's son! Why scorn'st thou at Sir Robert?
He is Sir Robert's son, and so art thou.
230 *Bastard.* James Gurney, wilt thou give us leave awhile?
Gurney. Good leave, good Philip.
Bastard.   Philip sparrow! James,
There's toys abroad; anon I'll tell thee more.

Exit James.

Madam, I was not old Sir Robert's son.
Sir Robert might have eat his part in me
235 Upon Good Friday and ne'er broke his fast.
Sir Robert could do well — marry, to confess —
Could he get me! Sir Robert could not do it.
We know his handiwork. Therefore, good mother,
To whom am I beholding for these limbs?
240 Sir Robert never holp to make this leg.
Lady Faulconbridge. Hast thou conspirèd with thy brother too,
That for thine own gain shouldst defend mine honor?
What means this scorn, thou most untoward knave?
Bastard. Knight, knight, good mother, Basilisco-like.
245 What! I am dubbed; I have it on my shoulder.
But, mother, I am not Sir Robert's son;
I have disclaimed Sir Robert and my land;
Legitimation, name, and all is gone.
Then, good my mother, let me know my father;
250 Some proper man I hope; who was it, mother?

231 *Philip sparrow* (since he has just been knighted, he objects to being
called merely Philip, the common name for a sparrow) 232 *toys* rumors
236–37 *Sir Robert . . . get me* (he is incredulous at the suggestion that
one like Sir Robert might be his father) 239 *beholding* indebted 240 *holp*
helped 243 *untoward* ill-mannered 244 *Basilisco-like* (the Bastard mocks
himself by comparing himself to Basilisco, the cowardly, braggart knight
in *Soliman and Perseda*, an old play probably by Thomas Kyd) 245 *dubbed*
made a knight 250 *proper* handsome

Lady Faulconbridge. Hast thou denied thyself a Faulcon-
    bridge?

Bastard. As faithfully as I deny the devil.

Lady Faulconbridge. King Richard Cordelion was thy father.
    By long and vehement suit I was seduced
    To make room for him in my husband's bed.   255
    Heaven lay not my transgression to my charge!
    Thou art the issue of my dear offense,
    Which was so strongly urged past my defense.

Bastard. Now, by this light, were I to get again,
    Madam, I would not wish a better father.   260
    Some sins do bear their privilege on earth,
    And so doth yours; your fault was not your folly.
    Needs must you lay your heart at his dispose,
    Subjected tribute to commanding love,
    Against whose fury and unmatchèd force   265
    The aweless lion could not wage the fight,
    Nor keep his princely heart from Richard's hand.
    He that perforce robs lions of their hearts
    May easily win a woman's. Ay, my mother,
    With all my heart I thank thee for my father!   270
    Who lives and dares but say thou didst not well
    When I was got, I'll send his soul to hell.
    Come, lady, I will show thee to my kin,
    And they shall say, when Richard me begot,
    If thou hadst said him nay, it had been sin.   275
    Who says it was, he lies; I say 'twas not.   *Exeunt.*

258 *urged . . . defense* forced in spite of my protests   259 *get* be conceived
261 *do bear . . . earth* are allowed on earth but not in heaven   263 *dispose*
disposal   266 *aweless lion* (King Richard, according to legend, had slain a
lion by thrusting his hand down its throat and tearing out its heart, which
he then ate; hence his nickname)

II, i *Enter before Angiers, Philip, King of France, Lewis,*
   [the] Dauphin, Austria, Constance, Arthur [and
   Attendants].

King Philip. Before Angiers well met, brave Austria.
 Arthur, that great forerunner of thy blood,
 Richard, that robbed the lion of his heart
 And fought the holy wars in Palestine,
5 By this brave duke came early to his grave;
 And for amends to his posterity,
 At our importance hither is he come
 To spread his colors, boy, in thy behalf,
 And to rebuke the usurpation
10 Of thy unnatural uncle, English John.
 Embrace him, love him, give him welcome
  hither.
Arthur. God shall forgive you Cordelion's death
 The rather that you give his offspring life,
 Shadowing their right under your wings of war.
15 I give you welcome with a powerless hand,
 But with a heart full of unstainèd love.
 Welcome before the gates of Angiers, duke.
Lewis. A noble boy! Who would not do thee right?
Austria. Upon thy cheek lay I this zealous kiss,
20 As seal to this indenture of my love,
 That to my home I will no more return
 Till Angiers and the right thou hast in France,
 Together with that pale, that white-faced shore,
 Whose foot spurns back the ocean's roaring tides

II, i, 2 *forerunner of thy blood* ancestor (Arthur was actually the nephew
of Richard, son of his brother Geoffrey) 5 *brave duke* Austria (although
Richard actually was killed before the castle of the Viscount Limoges;
Shakespeare, following his source, combines the two characters) 7 *importance* request 14 *Shadowing* sheltering 20 *indenture* sealed contract

And coops from other lands her islanders, 25
Even till that England, hedged in with the main,
That water-wallèd bulwark, still secure
And confident from foreign purposes,
Even till that utmost corner of the west
Salute thee for her king. Till then, fair boy, 30
Will I not think of home, but follow arms.
Constance. O, take his mother's thanks, a widow's thanks,
Till your strong hand shall help to give him strength
To make a more requital to your love.
Austria. The peace of heaven is theirs that lift their swords 35
In such a just and charitable war.
King Philip. Well then, to work; our cannon shall be bent
Against the brows of this resisting town.
Call for our chiefest men of discipline,
To cull the plots of best advantages. 40
We'll lay before this town our royal bones,
Wade to the market-place in Frenchmen's blood,
But we will make it subject to this boy.
Constance. Stay for an answer to your embassy,
Lest unadvised you stain your swords with blood. 45
My Lord Chatillion may from England bring
That right in peace which here we urge in war,
And then we shall repent each drop of blood
That hot rash haste so indirectly shed.

Enter Chatillion.

King Philip. A wonder, lady! Lo, upon thy wish, 50
Our messenger, Chatillion, is arrived!

25 *coops* encloses for protection 27 *still* forever 34 *more* greater 37 *bent*
directed 39 *discipline* military training or experience 40 *cull . . . ad-*
vantages select the most suitable locations for placing cannons 45 *unad-*
vised unwisely, without adequate consideration 49 *indirectly* unjustly

What England says, say briefly, gentle lord;
We coldly pause for thee; Chatillion, speak.
Chatillion. Then turn your forces from this paltry siege
55 And stir them up against a mightier task.
England, impatient of your just demands,
Hath put himself in arms. The adverse winds,
Whose leisure I have stayed, have given him time
To land his legions all as soon as I.
60 His marches are expedient to this town,
His forces strong, his soldiers confident.
With him along is come the mother-queen,
An Ate, stirring him to blood and strife;
With her her niece, the Lady Blanch of Spain;
65 With them a bastard of the king's deceased;
And all th' unsettled humors of the land,
Rash, inconsiderate, fiery voluntaries,
With ladies' faces and fierce dragons' spleens,
Have sold their fortunes at their native homes,
70 Bearing their birthrights proudly on their backs,
To make a hazard of new fortunes here.
In brief, a braver choice of dauntless spirits
Than now the English bottoms have waft o'er
Did never float upon the swelling tide,
75 To do offense and scathe in Christendom.
The interruption of their churlish drums
Cuts off more circumstance; they are at hand.

                                    Drum beats.
To parley or to fight, therefore prepare.

53 *coldly* calmly   58 *stayed* waited for   60 *expedient to* hastening towards
63 *Ate* the Greek goddess of mischief and vengeance   66 *unsettled humors*
restless disgruntled men   67 *voluntaries* volunteers   68 *dragons' spleens* hot
tempers (since the spleen was regarded as the seat of the passions)   70 *Bearing . . . backs* having sold their estates to purchase armor   73 *bottoms* ships
75 *scathe* harm   76 *churlish* lowly, inferior   77 *circumstance* details

King Philip. How much unlooked for is this expedition!
Austria. By how much unexpected, by so much   80
  We must awake endeavor for defense,
  For courage mounteth with occasion.
  Let them be welcome then; we are prepared.

Enter King [John] of England, Bastard, Queen [Elinor],
  Blanch, Pembroke, and others.

King John. Peace be to France, if France in peace permit
  Our just and lineal entrance to our own.   85
  If not, bleed France, and peace ascend to heaven,
  Whiles we, God's wrathful agent, do correct
  Their proud contempt that beats His peace to heaven.
King Philip. Peace be to England, if that war return
  From France to England, there to live in peace.   90
  England we love, and for that England's sake
  With burden of our armor here we sweat.
  This toil of ours should be a work of thine,
  But thou from loving England art so far
  That thou hast under-wrought his lawful king,   95
  Cut off the sequence of posterity,
  Outfacèd infant state, and done a rape
  Upon the maiden virtue of the crown.
  Look here upon thy brother Geoffrey's face.
  These eyes, these brows, were molded out of his;   100
  This little abstract doth contain that large

79 *expedition* haste   82 *occasion* emergency   85 *lineal* due by right of descent   87 *correct* punish   91 *England's* i.e. Arthur's (since Philip takes him to be the lawful king of England)   93 *This toil . . . thine* i.e. John should be fighting for Arthur's cause rather than against him   95 *under-wrought* undermined   96 *sequence of posterity* hereditary succession to the throne   97 *Outfaced infant state* intimidated a child king   101–3 *little abstract . . . volume* i.e. Arthur as a child is like a shortened edition of his father, Geoffrey, but in time he will grow to be as complete a volume (of virtues) as his father was

41

Which died in Geoffrey, and the hand of time
Shall draw this brief into as huge a volume.
That Geoffrey was thy elder brother born,
105   And this his son. England was Geoffrey's right
And this is Geoffrey's in the name of God.
How comes it then that thou art called a king,
When living blood doth in these temples beat,
Which owe the crown that thou o'ermasterest?

King John. From whom hast thou this great commission,
110   France,
To draw my answer from thy articles?

King Philip. From that supernal judge that stirs good
      thoughts
In any breast of strong authority,
To look into the blots and stains of right.
115   That judge hath made me guardian to this boy,
Under whose warrant I impeach thy wrong
And by whose help I mean to chastise it.

King John. Alack, thou dost usurp authority.

King Philip. Excuse it is to beat usurping down.

120 *Elinor.* Who is it thou dost call usurper, France?

Constance. Let me make answer: thy usurping son.

Elinor. Out, insolent! Thy bastard shall be king
That thou mayst be a queen and check the world!

Constance. My bed was ever to thy son as true
125   As thine was to thy husband, and this boy
Liker in feature to his father Geoffrey
Than thou and John in manners, being as like

106 *this* (a famous crux; may refer to Arthur, John's crown, or the city of
Angiers, depending upon what the actor indicates by his arm)   109 *owe*
own   *o'ermasterest* usurpest   111 *draw ... articles* demand that I answer
your charges   112 *supernal* heavenly   116 *impeach* accuse   123 *queen*
(with play on 'quean,' whore)   *check* control (with possible allusion to
game of chess)

As rain to water, or devil to his dam.
My boy a bastard! By my soul I think
His father never was so true begot.   130
It cannot be and if thou wert his mother.

Elinor. There's a good mother, boy, that blots thy father.

Constance. There's a good grandam, boy, that would blot
  thee.

Austria. Peace!

Bastard.   Hear the crier.

Austria.   What the devil art thou?

Bastard. One that will play the devil, sir, with you,   135
  An 'a may catch your hide and you alone.
  You are the hare of whom the proverb goes,
  Whose valor plucks dead lions by the beard.
  I'll smoke your skin-coat, an I catch you right.
  Sirrah, look to 't; i' faith, I will, i' faith.   140

Blanch. O well did he become that lion's robe,
  That did disrobe the lion of that robe!

Bastard. It lies as sightly on the back of him
  As great Alcides' shows upon an ass.
  But, ass, I'll take that burden from your back,   145
  Or lay on that shall make your shoulders crack.

Austria. What cracker is this same that deafs our ears
  With this abundance of superfluous breath?
  King Philip, determine what we shall do straight.

King Philip. Women and fools, break off your conference. 150

---

128 *dam* mother 132 *blots* slanders 133 *grandam* grandmother 134 *Hear
the crier* (the Bastard mocks Austria by likening him to the town crier
who called for silence in the courts) 136 *An 'a* if he 137 *the proverb*
i.e. 'hares may pull dead lions by the beard' (it occurs in the *Adagia* of
Erasmus) 139 *smoke your skin-coat* thrash you (alluding also to King
Richard's lion skin, which Austria is wearing) 143 *sightly* appropriately
144 *Alcides* Hercules, who wore the skin of the Nemean lion he had slain
147 *cracker* boaster 149 *straight* immediately 150 *fools* children

43

King John, this is the very sum of all:
England and Ireland, Angiers, Touraine, Maine,
In right of Arthur do I claim of thee.
Wilt thou resign them and lay down thy arms?
155 *King John.* My life as soon! I do defy thee, France.
Arthur of Britain, yield thee to my hand,
And out of my dear love I'll give thee more
Than e'er the coward hand of France can win.
Submit thee, boy.
Elinor.   Come to thy grandam, child.
160 *Constance.* Do, child, go to it grandam, child;
Give grandam kingdom, and it grandam will
Give it a plum, a cherry, and a fig.
There's a good grandam.
Arthur.   Good my mother, peace!
I would that I were low laid in my grave.
165 I am not worth this coil that's made for me.
Elinor. His mother shames him so, poor boy, he weeps.
Constance. Now shame upon you, whe'r she does or no!
His grandam's wrongs, and not his mother's shames,
Draws those heaven-moving pearls from his poor eyes,
170 Which heaven shall take in nature of a fee.
Ay, with these crystal beads heaven shall be bribed
To do him justice and revenge on you.
Elinor. Thou monstrous slanderer of heaven and earth!
Constance. Thou monstrous injurer of heaven and earth!
175 Call not me slanderer; thou and thine usurp
The dominations, royalties, and rights
Of this oppressèd boy. This is thy eldest son's son,

152 *Angiers* (here confused with Anjou) 160–63 *Do . . . grandam*
(Constance uses baby talk to ridicule Elinor's invitation) 165 *coil* fuss
167 *whe'r* whether 169 *Draws* draw *pearls* tears 176 *dominations* sov-
ereignties 177 *eldest son's son* oldest grandson, a biblical form (not son of
your oldest son, which Arthur was not)

Infortunate in nothing but in thee.
Thy sins are visited in this poor child;
The canon of the law is laid on him,   180
Being but the second generation
Removèd from thy sin-conceiving womb.
King John. Bedlam, have done.
Constance.   I have but this to say,
That he is not only plaguèd for her sin,
But God hath made her sin and her the plague   185
On this removèd issue, plagued for her
And with her plague; her sin his injury,
Her injury the beadle to her sin,
All punished in the person of this child,
And all for her; a plague upon her.   190
Elinor. Thou unadvisèd scold, I can produce
A will that bars the title of thy son.
Constance. Ay, who doubts that? A will! A wicked
will;
A woman's will; a cankered grandam's will!
King Philip. Peace, lady! Pause, or be more temperate. 195
It ill beseems this presence to cry aim
To these ill-tunèd repetitions.
Some trumpet summon hither to the walls

---

178 *Infortunate* unfortunate   179 *visited* punished   180 *canon of the law*
i.e. that the sins of parents be visited upon their children to the third
and fourth generation   183 *Bedlam* lunatic   184–90 *That. . . upon her* (a
perhaps intentionally obscure passage, the sense being that Arthur is being
punished for the sin of Elinor—her giving birth to John, whom Constance
is calling a bastard—by the very presence of Elinor and John, that they
are laying the scourge upon him which should be laid upon Elinor)
186 *removèd issue* distant descendant   188 *beadle* a parish official who
meted out corporal punishment, to prostitutes in particular   191 *unadvisèd*
rash   192 *A will* (the last testament of King Richard I, which named his
brother John heir to the throne)   194 *cankered* malignant   196 *cry aim*
give encouragement   198 *trumpet* trumpeter

These men of Angiers. Let us hear them speak
200 Whose title they admit, Arthur's or John's.

Trumpet sounds. Enter a Citizen upon the walls.

Citizen. Who is it that hath warned us to the walls?
King Philip. 'Tis France, for England.
King John.   England for itself.
You men of Angiers, and my loving subjects —
King Philip. You loving men of Angiers, Arthur's subjects,
205 Our trumpet called you to this gentle parle —
King John. For our advantage; therefore hear us first.
These flags of France, that are advancèd here
Before the eye and prospect of your town,
Have hither marched to your endamagement.
210 The cannons have their bowels full of wrath,
And ready mounted are they to spit forth
Their iron indignation 'gainst your walls.
All preparation for a bloody siege
And merciless proceeding by these French
215 Confront your city's eyes, your winking gates,
And but for our approach those sleeping stones,
That as a waist doth girdle you about,
By the compulsion of their ordinance
By this time from their fixèd beds of lime
220 Had been dishabited, and wide havoc made
For bloody power to rush upon your peace.
But on the sight of us your lawful king,
Who painfully with much expedient march
Have brought a countercheck before your gates,

201 *warned* summoned 205 *parle* conference 207 *advancèd* raised
208 *prospect* view 209 *endamagement* injury 215 *winking* closed as in
sleep 217 *waist* belt *doth* do 218 *ordinance* artillery 220 *dishabited*
dislodged 223 *painfully* laboriously *expedient* speedy

To save unscratched your city's threat'ned cheeks,   225
Behold, the French amazed vouchsafe a parle;
And now, instead of bullets wrapped in fire,
To make a shaking fever in your walls,
They shoot but calm words folded up in smoke,
To make a faithless error in your ears.   230
Which trust accordingly, kind citizens,
And let us in, your king, whose labored spirits,
Forwearied in this action of swift speed,
Craves harborage within your city walls.
King Philip. When I have said, make answer to us both.   235
Lo! In this right hand, whose protection
Is most divinely vowed upon the right
Of him it holds, stands young Plantagenet,
Son to the elder brother of this man,
And king o'er him and all that he enjoys.   240
For this downtrodden equity we tread
In warlike march these greens before your town,
Being no further enemy to you
Than the constraint of hospitable zeal,
In the relief of this oppressèd child,   245
Religiously provokes. Be pleasèd then
To pay that duty which you truly owe
To him that owes it, namely this young prince;
And then our arms, like to a muzzled bear,
Save in aspect, hath all offense sealed up.   250
Our cannons' malice vainly shall be spent
Against th' invulnerable clouds of heaven,
And with a blessèd and unvexed retire,

230 *faithless* perfidious, disloyal *error* falsehood 232 *labored* oppressed by
labor 233 *Forwearied* tired out *action* campaign 234 *harborage* shelter,
acceptance 236 *In this right hand* led by my right hand 238 *holds* supports
240 *enjoys* possesses 242 *greens* grassy ground outside the city gates 248
owes owns 250 *Save in aspect* except for appearance 253 *retire* withdrawal

With unhacked swords and helmets all unbruised,
255 We will bear home that lusty blood again
Which here we came to spout against your town,
And leave your children, wives, and you, in peace.
But if you fondly pass our proffered offer,
'Tis not the roundure of your old-faced walls
260 Can hide you from our messengers of war.
Though all these English and their discipline
Were harbored in their rude circumference.
Then tell us, shall your city call us lord,
In that behalf which we have challenged it?
265 Or shall we give the signal to our rage
And stalk in blood to our possession?
Citizen. In brief, we are the King of England's subjects.
For him, and in his right, we hold this town.
King John. Acknowledge then the king, and let me in.
270 *Citizen.* That can we not; but he that proves the king,
To him will we prove loyal. Till that time
Have we rammed up our gates against the world.
King John. Doth not the crown of England prove the king?
And if not that, I bring you witnesses,
275 Twice fifteen thousand hearts of England's breed —
Bastard. Bastards, and else.
King John. To verify our title with their lives.
King Philip. As many and as well-born bloods as those —
Bastard. Some bastards, too.
280 *King Philip.* Stand in his face to contradict his claim.
Citizen. Till you compound whose right is worthiest,
We for the worthiest hold the right from both.

---

258 *fondly pass* foolishly ignore   259 *roundure* circumference   260 *messengers of war* cannon balls   261 *discipline* military skill   264 *which* in which
270 *proves* is proved   276 *and else* and otherwise   278 *bloods* men of mettle, and of good family   280 *in his face* opposing him   281 *compound* agree

48

King John. Then God forgive the sins of all those souls
  That to their everlasting residence,
  Before the dew of evening fall, shall fleet,   285
  In dreadful trial of our kingdom's king!
King Philip. Amen, amen! Mount, chevaliers! To arms!
Bastard. Saint George, that swinged the dragon, and e'er
    since
  Sits on's horseback at mine hostess' door,
  Teach us some fence! *[to Austria]* Sirrah, were I at home 290
  At your den, sirrah, with your lioness,
  I would set an ox head to your lion's hide,
  And make a monster of you.
Austria.   Peace! No more.
Bastard. O tremble, for you hear the lion roar.
King John. Up higher to the plain, where we'll set forth 295
  In best appointment all our regiments.
Bastard. Speed then, to take advantage of the field.
King Philip. It shall be so; and at the other hill
  Command the rest to stand. God, and our right! *Exeunt.*

    *Here after excursions, enter the Herald of France with
        Trumpets, to the gates.*

French Herald. You men of Angiers, open wide your gates, 300
  And let young Arthur, Duke of Britain, in,
  Who by the hand of France this day hath made
  Much work for tears in many an English mother,
  Whose sons lie scattered on the bleeding ground.
  Many a widow's husband grovelling lies,   305
  Coldly embracing the discolored earth,

285 *fleet* pass away 288 *swinged* thrashed 290 *fence* swordsmanship, defense 291 *lioness* (a slang expression for whore) 292–93 *set . . . you* cause you to grow the horns of a cuckold (a common joke of the time) 305 *grovelling* prone, on his belly

49

And victory with little loss doth play
Upon the dancing banners of the French,
Who are at hand, triumphantly displayed,
310 To enter conquerors and to proclaim
Arthur of Britain England's king and yours.

Enter English Herald, with Trumpet.

English Herald. Rejoice, you men of Angiers, ring your
        bells.
King John, your king and England's, doth approach,
Commander of this hot malicious day.
315 Their armors, that marched hence so silver-bright,
Hither return all gilt with Frenchmen's blood.
There stuck no plume in any English crest
That is removèd by a staff of France.
Our colors do return in those same hands
320 That did display them when we first marched forth,
And like a jolly troop of huntsmen come
Our lusty English, all with purpled hands
Dyed in the dying slaughter of their foes.
Open your gates and give the victors way.
325 *Citizen.* Heralds, from off our towers we might behold,
From first to last, the onset and retire
Of both your armies, whose equality
By our best eyes cannot be censurèd.
Blood hath bought blood, and blows have answered
        blows,

---

309 *displayed* deployed, spread out   314 *hot malicious* hotly and violently
fought   316 *gilt* made red   318 *staff* shaft of a spear   322 *purpled* bloody
323 *Dyed . . . foes* (it was a custom for hunters to dip their hands in the
blood of the slain deer)   325 *Citizen* (in the folio this speech is given to
Hubert, identifying him with the citizen of Angiers)   326 *retire* retreat
328 *censurèd* estimated

Strength matched with strength, and power confronted
   power.   330
Both are alike, and both alike we like.
One must prove greatest. While they weigh so even,
We hold our town for neither, yet for both.

Enter the two Kings, with their powers, at several doors.

King John. France, hast thou yet more blood to cast away?
  Say, shall the current of our right run on?   335
  Whose passage, vexed with thy impediment,
  Shall leave his native channel and o'erswell
  With course disturbed even thy confining shores,
  Unless thou let his silver water keep
  A peaceful progress to the ocean.   340
King Philip. England, thou hast not saved one drop of
   blood
  In this hot trial more than we of France;
  Rather, lost more. And by this hand I swear,
  That sways the earth this climate overlooks,
  Before we will lay down our just-borne arms,   345
  We'll put thee down, 'gainst whom these arms we bear,
  Or add a royal number to the dead,
  Gracing the scroll that tells of this war's loss
  With slaughter couplèd to the name of kings.
Bastard. Ha, majesty! How high thy glory towers   350
  When the rich blood of kings is set on fire!
  O now doth death line his dead chaps with steel!
  The swords of soldiers are his teeth, his fangs;
  And now he feasts, mousing the flesh of men.
  In undetermined differences of kings.   355

344 *climate* portion of the sky 347 *royal number* a royal item on the
scroll bearing the official list of the dead 352 *chaps* jaws 354 *mousing*
tearing 355 *undetermined differences* unsettled quarrels

Why stand these royal fronts amazèd thus?
Cry 'havoc!', kings; back to the stainèd field,
You equal potents, fiery kindled spirits!
Then let confusion of one part confirm
360   The other's peace; till then, blows, blood, and death!
King John. Whose party do the townsmen yet admit?
King Philip. Speak, citizens, for England; who's your king?
Citizen. The King of England, when we know the king.
King Philip. Know him in us, that here hold up his right.
365   *King John.* In us, that are our own great deputy,
And bear possession of our person here,
Lord of our presence, Angiers, and of you.
Citizen. A greater power than we denies all this,
And till it be undoubted, we do lock
370   Our former scruple in our strong-barred gates,
Kinged of our fear, until our fears, resolved,
Be by some certain king purged and deposed.
Bastard. By heaven, these scroyles of Angiers flout you,
        kings,
And stand securely on their battlements
375   As in a theatre, whence they gape and point
At your industrious scenes and acts of death.
Your royal presences be ruled by me.
Do like the mutines of Jerusalem,
Be friends awhile and both conjointly bend
380   Your sharpest deeds of malice on this town.
By east and west let France and England mount
Their battering cannon chargèd to the mouths,

356 *fronts* faces (literally, foreheads) 357 *havoc* (this cry was a traditional signal for indiscriminate slaughter with no taking of prisoners)
358 *potents* powers 359 *confusion* defeat *part* party 361 *yet* now 371
Kinged of ruled by 373 *scroyles* scoundrels 378 *mutines of Jerusalem* (when
Jerusalem was besieged by the Emperor Titus, warring factions within the
city united in common struggle against the Romans) 379 *bend* direct

Till their soul-fearing clamors have brawled down
The flinty ribs of this contemptuous city.
I'd play incessantly upon these jades,   385
Even till unfencèd desolation
Leave them as naked as the vulgar air.
That done, dissever your united strengths,
And part your mingled colors once again;
Turn face to face and bloody point to point.   390
Then in a moment fortune shall cull forth
Out of one side her happy minion,
To whom in favor she shall give the day,
And kiss him with a glorious victory.
How like you this wild counsel, mighty states?   395
Smacks it not something of the policy?

King John. Now, by the sky that hangs above our heads,
I like it well. France, shall we knit our powers
And lay this Angiers even with the ground,
Then after fight who shall be king of it?   400

Bastard. And if thou hast the mettle of a king,
Being wronged as we are by this peevish town,
Turn thou the mouth of thy artillery,
As we will ours, against these saucy walls;
And when that we have dashed them to the ground,   405
Why then defy each other, and pell-mell
Make work upon ourselves, for heaven or hell.

King Philip. Let it be so. Say, where will you assault?

383 *brawled down* beaten down with noise   385 *play . . . jades* fire repeat-
edly upon these wretches   386 *unfencèd* defenseless   387 *naked* unarmed
vulgar common to all   391 *fortune* chance (commonly personified in medi-
eval and Renaissance literature as a fickle goddess)   392 *minion* sweetheart,
favorite   395 *states* kings   396 *policy* art of politics in pejorative sense,
involving trickery and deceit (the Bastard is rather naïvely boasting
of his ability as a politician)   402 *peevish* obstinate   406 *pell-mell* in
confusion

King John. We from the west will send destruction
410   Into this city's bosom.
Austria. I from the north.
King Philip.   Our thunder from the south
Shall rain their drift of bullets on this town.
Bastard. [*aside*] O prudent discipline! From north to south
Austria and France shoot in each other's mouth.
415   I'll stir them to it. Come, away, away!
Citizen. Hear us, great kings; vouchsafe a while to stay,
And I shall show you peace and fair-faced league,
Win you this city without stroke or wound,
Rescue those breathing lives to die in beds,
420   That here come sacrifices for the field.
Persever not, but hear me, mighty kings.
King John. Speak on with favor; we are bent to hear.
Citizen. That daughter there of Spain, the Lady Blanch,
Is near to England. Look upon the years
425   Of Lewis the Dauphin and that lovely maid.
If lusty love should go in quest of beauty,
Where should he find it fairer than in Blanch?
If zealous love should go in search of virtue,
Where should he find it purer than in Blanch?
430   If love ambitious sought a match of birth,
Whose veins bound richer blood than Lady Blanch?
Such as she is, in beauty, virtue, birth,
Is the young Dauphin every way complete.
If not complete of, say he is not she,
435   And she again wants nothing, to name want,

411 *thunder* cannon   412 *drift* rain   413 *discipline* military skill   422 *fa vor* permission   *bent* inclined   424 *near to England* a close relative of King John   428 *zealous love* holy love, as opposed to lust   431 *bound* con tain   433 *complete* perfect   434–36 *If . . . not he* (a type of word play in which Elizabethans delighted, the sense being that each requires the other to make his own perfection even more perfect)

If want it be not that she is not he.
He is the half part of a blessèd man,
Left to be finishèd by such as she,
And she a fair divided excellence,
Whose fulness of perfection lies in him.   440
O, two such silver currents when they join
Do glorify the banks that bound them in;
And two such shores to two such streams made one,
Two such controlling bounds shall you be, kings,
To these two princes, if you marry them.   445
This union shall do more than battery can
To our fast-closèd gates; for at this match,
With swifter spleen than powder can enforce,
The mouth of passage shall we fling wide ope,
And give you entrance; but without this match,   450
The sea enragèd is not half so deaf,
Lions more confident, mountains and rocks
More free from motion, no, not death himself
In mortal fury half so peremptory,
As we to keep this city.
Bastard.   Here's a stay,   455
That shakes the rotten carcase of old death
Out of his rags! Here's a large mouth, indeed,
That spits forth death and mountains, rocks and seas,
Talks as familiarly of roaring lions
As maids of thirteen do of puppy-dogs.   460
What cannoneer begot this lusty blood?
He speaks plain cannon fire and smoke and bounce.
He gives the bastinado with his tongue.

441 *silver currents* (marriage was often celebrated in Elizabethan love
poetry as a joining of two streams of water)   447 *match* (1) marriage (2) the
match which fires the cannon   448 *spleen* violent energy   454 *peremptory*
determined   455 *stay* obstacle   457 *rags* (death was often portrayed in me-
dieval art as a skeleton clad in rags)   462 *bounce* bang   463 *bastinado* a beat-
ing with a stick

Our ears are cudgelled; not a word of his
465   But buffets better than a fist of France.
'Zounds! I was never so bethumped with words
Since I first called my brother's father dad.
    Elinor. Son, list to this conjunction, make this match.
Give with our niece a dowry large enough,
470   For by this knot thou shalt so surely tie
Thy now unsured assurance to the crown
That yon green boy shall have no sun to ripe
The bloom that promiseth a mighty fruit.
I see a yielding in the looks of France.
475   Mark how they whisper. Urge them while their souls
Are capable of this ambition,
Lest zeal, now melted by the windy breath
Of soft petitions, pity, and remorse,
Cool and congeal again to what it was.
480   *Citizen.* Why answer not the double majesties
This friendly treaty of our threat'ned town?
    King Philip. Speak England first, that hath been forward first
To speak unto this city. What say you?
    King John. If that the Dauphin there, thy princely son,
485   Can in this book of beauty read 'I love,'
Her dowry shall weigh equal with a queen;
For Angiers and fair Touraine, Maine, Poitiers,
And all that we upon this side the sea,
Except this city now by us besieged,
490   Find liable to our crown and dignity,

466 *'Zounds* by God's wounds   468 *list* pay close heed   471 *unsured* insecure   476 *capable of* susceptible to   *ambition* desire to come to terms   477–79 *Lest . . . what it was* lest the French king's desire to help Arthur, now melted by the pleas of the citizen of Angiers, become as firm as it was before   478 *remorse* compassion   481 *treaty* proposal   487 *Angiers* i.e. Anjou   490 *liable* subject

Shall gild her bridal bed and make her rich
In titles, honors, and promotions,
As she in beauty, education, blood,
Holds hand with any princess of the world.

King Philip. What sayst thou, boy? Look in the lady's face. 495

Lewis. I do, my lord, and in her eye I find
A wonder or a wondrous miracle,
The shadow of myself formed in her eye,
Which, being but the shadow of your son,
Becomes a sun, and makes your son a shadow. 500
I do protest I never loved myself
Till now infixèd I beheld myself,
Drawn in the flattering table of her eye.

                    Whispers with Blanch.

Bastard. Drawn in the flattering table of her eye!
Hanged in the frowning wrinkle of her brow! 505
And quartered in her heart! He doth espy
Himself love's traitor; this is pity now,
That hanged and drawn and quartered, there should be
In such a love so vile a lout as he.

Blanch. My uncle's will in this respect is mine. 510
If he see aught in you that makes him like,
That anything he sees which moves his liking,
I can with ease translate it to my will;
Or if you will, to speak more properly,
I will enforce it easily to my love. 515
Further I will not flatter you, my lord,
That all I see in you is worthy love,

---

494 *Holds hand with* equals   498 *shadow* reflection (the elaborate **sun-mis-tress** conceit, very common in Shakespeare's day, emphasizes the artificiality of the wooing)   503 *Drawn* pictured *table* flat surface on which a picture is painted   504 *Drawn* (with a quibble on the sense of disembowelled)   506 *quartered* lodged (with quibble; Elizabethan traitors were hanged, drawn, and quartered)   513 *translate it to my will* cause it to suit my own desires

    Than this: that nothing do I see in you,
    Though churlish thoughts themselves should be your
        judge,
520   That I can find should merit any hate.
    King John. What say these young ones? What say you, my
      niece?
    Blanch. That she is bound in honor still to do
    What you in wisdom still vouchsafe to say.
    King John. Speak then, Prince Dauphin. Can you love this
      lady?
525 *Lewis.* Nay, ask me if I can refrain from love,
    For I do love her most unfeignèdly.
    King John. Then do I give Volquessen, Touraine, Maine,
    Poitiers, and Anjou, these five provinces,
    With her to thee; and this addition more,
530   Full thirty thousand marks of English coin.
    Philip of France, if thou be pleased withal,
    Command thy son and daughter to join hands.
    King Philip. It likes us well. Young princes, close your
      hands.
    Austria. And your lips too, for I am well assured
535   That I did so when I was first assured.
    King Philip. Now, citizens of Angiers, ope your gates,
    Let in that amity which you have made,
    For at Saint Mary's chapel presently
    The rites of marriage shall be solemnized.
540   Is not the Lady Constance in this troop?
    I know she is not, for this match made up
    Her presence would have interrupted much.
    Where is she and her son? Tell me, who knows.
    Lewis. She is sad and passionate at your highness' tent.

519 *churlish* miserly (of praise)   522, 523 *still* always   533 *likes* pleases
535 *assured* betrothed   537 *that amity* those friends   544 *passionate* angry

King Philip. And, by my faith, this league that we have
        made   545
  Will give her sadness very little cure.
  Brother of England, how may we content
  This widow lady? In her right we came,
  Which we, God knows, have turned another way,
  To our own vantage.
King John.   We will heal up all,   550
  For we'll create young Arthur Duke of Britain
  And Earl of Richmond, and this rich fair town
  We make him lord of. Call the Lady Constance.
  Some speedy messenger bid her repair
  To our solemnity. I trust we shall,   555
  If not fill up the measure of her will,
  Yet in some measure satisfy her so,
  That we shall stop her exclamation.
  Go we, as well as haste will suffer us,
  To this unlooked for, unprepared pomp.   560
                        Exeunt [all but the Bastard].
Bastard. Mad world! Mad kings! Mad composition!
  John, to stop Arthur's title in the whole,
  Hath willingly departed with a part,
  And France, whose armor conscience buckled on,
  Whom zeal and charity brought to the field   565
  As God's own soldier, rounded in the ear
  With that same purpose-changer, that sly devil,
  That broker, that still breaks the pate of faith,
  That daily break-vow, he that wins of all,
  Of kings, of beggars, old men, young men, maids,   570

555 *our solemnity* the wedding ceremony 558 *stop her exclamation* silence
her loud complaints 559 *suffer* permit 561 *composition* agreement 563 *departed with* relinquished 566 *rounded* whispered 567 *With* by 568 *broker*
go-between (in a pejorative sense, as a pander)

Who, having no external thing to lose
But the word 'maid,' cheats the poor maid of that,
That smooth-faced gentleman, tickling commodity,
Commodity, the bias of the world;
575 The world, who of itself is peisèd well,
Made to run even upon even ground,
Till this advantage, this vile-drawing bias,
This sway of motion, this commodity,
Makes it take head from all indifferency,
580 From all direction, purpose, course, intent.
And this same bias, this commodity,
This bawd, this broker, this all-changing word,
Clapped on the outward eye of fickle France,
Hath drawn him from his own determined aid,
585 From a resolved and honorable war,
To a most base and vile-concluded peace.
And why rail I on this commodity?
But for because he hath not wooed me yet.
Not that I have the power to clutch my hand
590 When his fair angels would salute my palm,
But for my hand, as unattempted yet,
Like a poor beggar, raileth on the rich.
Well, whiles I am a beggar, I will rail
And say there is no sin but to be rich;
595 And being rich, my virtue then shall be
To say there is no vice but beggary.

571 *Who* i.e. the maids 573 *tickling* flattering *commodity* self-interest
574 *bias* the weight in a bowling ball which causes it to curve 575 *peisèd*
balanced, weighted 577 *vile-drawing* leading into evil 579 *take . . . indifferency* rush away from all moderation 583 *eye* (1) vision (2) that
part of the bowl where the bias was placed *France* (Philip is now the
bowl drawn aside by the bias in his eye; the outward eye is distinguished
from the inner, or conscience) 585 *resolved* already decided upon 588 *But
for because* merely because 590 *angels* Elizabethan coins bearing the relief
of an angel 591 *unattempted* untempted

Since kings break faith upon commodity,
Gain, be my lord, for I will worship thee!   *Exit.*

Enter Constance, Arthur, and Salisbury.   III, i

Constance. Gone to be married! Gone to swear a peace!
   False blood to false blood joined! Gone to be friends!
   Shall Lewis have Blanch, and Blanch those provinces?
   It is not so; thou hast misspoke, misheard.
   Be well advised, tell o'er thy tale again.   5
   It cannot be; thou dost but say 'tis so.
   I trust I may not trust thee, for thy word
   Is but the vain breath of a common man.
   Believe me, I do not believe thee, man;
   I have a king's oath to the contrary.   10
   Thou shalt be punished for thus frighting me,
   For I am sick and capable of fears,
   Oppressed with wrongs, and therefore full of fears,
   A widow, husbandless, subject to fears,
   A woman, naturally born to fears;   15
   And though thou now confess thou didst but jest,
   With my vexed spirits I cannot take a truce,
   But they will quake and tremble all this day.
   What dost thou mean by shaking of thy head?
   Why dost thou look so sadly on my son?   20
   What means that hand upon that breast of thine?
   Why holds thine eye that lamentable rheum,
   Like a proud river peering o'er his bounds?

597 *upon* because of   III, i, 17 *take a truce* make peace   22 *rheum* moisture,
tears   23 *peering o'er* overflowing

Be these sad signs confirmers of thy words?
25   Then speak again, not all thy former tale,
But this one word, whether thy tale be true.
Salisbury. As true as I believe you think them false
That give you cause to prove my saying true.
Constance. O if thou teach me to believe this sorrow,
30   Teach thou this sorrow how to make me die!
And let belief and life encounter so
As doth the fury of two desperate men
Which in the very meeting fall and die.
Lewis marry Blanch! O boy, then where art thou?
35   France friend with England, what becomes of me?
Fellow, be gone! I cannot brook thy sight.
This news hath made thee a most ugly man.
Salisbury. What other harm have I, good lady, done,
But spoke the harm that is by others done?
40 *Constance.* Which harm within itself so heinous is
As it makes harmful all that speak of it.
Arthur. I do beseech you, madam, be content.
Constance. If thou that bid'st me be content wert grim,
Ugly and slanderous to thy mother's womb,
45   Full of unpleasing blots and sightless stains,
Lame, foolish, crooked, swart, prodigious,
Patched with foul moles and eye-offending marks,
I would not care, I then would be content,
For then I should not love thee; no, nor thou
50   Become thy great birth, nor deserve a crown.
But thou art fair, and at thy birth, dear boy,
Nature and fortune joined to make thee great.
Of nature's gifts thou mayst with lilies boast

27 *them* i.e. the French king and his advisers 42 *content* calm, quiet 44 *slanderous* a disgrace 45 *blots* blemishes *sightless* unsightly 46 *swart* of dark complexion *prodigious* deformed, bearing the mark of the Devil

And with the half-blown rose. But fortune, O!
She is corrupted, changed, and won from thee.   55
Sh' adulterates hourly with thine uncle John,
And with her golden hand hath plucked on France
To tread down fair respect of sovereignty,
And made his majesty the bawd to theirs.
France is a bawd to fortune and King John,   60
That strumpet fortune, that usurping John!
Tell me, thou fellow, is not France forsworn?
Envenom him with words, or get thee gone
And leave those woes alone which I alone
Am bound to underbear.

Salisbury.   Pardon me, madam,   65
I may not go without you to the kings.

Constance. Thou mayst, thou shalt; I will not go with thee.
I will instruct my sorrows to be proud,
For grief is proud and makes his owner stoop.
To me and to the state of my great grief   70
Let kings assemble, for my grief's so great
That no supporter but the huge firm earth
Can hold it up. Here I and sorrows sit.
Here is my throne; bid kings come bow to it.
                          [Seats herself on the ground.]

Enter King John, [King Philip of] France, [Lewis, the]
   Dauphin, Blanch, Elinor, Philip [the Bastard], Austria,
   Constance [and Attendants].

King Philip. 'Tis true, fair daughter, and this blessèd day   75
   Ever in France shall be kept festival.

56 *adulterates* (1) commits adultery (2) changes, shows her fickleness 57
with her golden hand by bribery *plucked on* incited 63 *Envenom* vituperate
65 *underbear* endure 69 *grief . . . stoop* (Constance sees herself as the
slave of the grief which she possesses but which masters her) 70 *state*
royal court 76 *festival* as a holiday

To solemnize this day the glorious sun
Stays in his course and plays the alchemist,
Turning with splendor of his precious eye
80   The meagre cloddy earth to glittering gold.
The yearly course that brings this day about
Shall never see it but a holy day.
Constance. [*rising*] A wicked day, and not a holy day!
What hath this day deserved? What hath it done
85   That it in golden letters should be set
Among the high tides in the calendar?
Nay, rather turn this day out of the week,
This day of shame, oppression, perjury.
Or, if it must stand still, let wives with child
90   Pray that their burdens may not fall this day,
Lest that their hopes prodigiously be crossed.
But on this day let seamen fear no wrack;
No bargains break that are not this day made;
This day all things begun come to ill end;
95   Yea, faith itself to hollow falsehood change!
King Philip. By heaven, lady, you shall have no cause
To curse the fair proceedings of this day.
Have I not pawned to you my majesty?
Constance. You have beguiled me with a counterfeit
100   Resembling majesty, which, being touched and tried,
Proves valueless. You are forsworn, forsworn.
You came in arms to spill mine enemies' blood,
But now in arms you strengthen it with yours.
The grappling vigor and rough frown of war

80 *meagre* barren 86 *high tides* great festivals 89 *stand still* remain 91
prodigiously be crossed be disappointed by the birth of a monster 92 *But*
except *wrack* shipwreck 98 *pawned* pledged 99 *counterfeit* false coin
100 *touched and tried* tested by being rubbed on a touchstone 102 *in arms*
wearing armor 103 *in arms* embracing one another *yours* your blood
relative, Lewis

Is cold in amity and painted peace, 105
And our oppression hath made up this league.
Arm, arm, you heavens, against these perjured kings!
A widow cries; be husband to me, heavens!
Let not the hours of this ungodly day
Wear out the day in peace; but, ere sunset, 110
Set armèd discord 'twixt these perjured kings!
Hear me! O, hear me!

Austria. Lady Constance, peace!

Constance. War! War! No peace! Peace is to me a war.
O, Lymoges! O, Austria! Thou dost shame
That bloody spoil. Thou slave, thou wretch, thou
    coward! 115
Thou little valiant, great in villainy!
Thou ever strong upon the stronger side!
Thou fortune's champion, that dost never fight
But when her humorous ladyship is by
To teach thee safety! Thou art perjured too, 120
And sooth'st up greatness. What a fool art thou,
A ramping fool, to brag and stamp and swear
Upon my party! Thou cold-blooded slave,
Hast thou not spoke like thunder on my side,
Been sworn my soldier, bidding me depend 125
Upon thy stars, thy fortune, and thy strength,
And dost thou now fall over to my foes?
Thou wear a lion's hide! Doff it for shame,
And hang a calfskin on those recreant limbs.

Austria. O that a man should speak those words to me! 130

105 *Is . . . peace* lies dead in a new friendship and pretended peace 106 *oppression* distress 115 *bloody spoil* i.e. the lion skin he wears 119 *humorous* fickle, capricious 121 *sooth'st up* flatterest 122 *ramping* rushing wildly about like a lion 123 *Upon my party* on my side 127 *fall over* desert 129 *calfskin* (material of which coats for household fools traditionally were made; alluding also to the cowardice of Austria) *recreant* cowardly

Bastard. And hang a calfskin on those recreant limbs.
Austria. Thou dar'st not say so, villain, for thy life.
Bastard. And hang a calfskin on those recreant limbs.
King John. We like not this; thou dost forget thyself.

Enter Pandulph.

135 *King Philip.* Here comes the holy legate of the Pope.
  Pandulph. Hail, you anointed deputies of heaven!
    To thee, King John, my holy errand is.
    I Pandulph, of fair Milan cardinal,
    And from Pope Innocent the legate here,
140 Do in his name religiously demand
    Why thou against the church, our holy mother,
    So wilfully dost spurn; and force perforce
    Keep Stephen Langton, chosen Archbishop
    Of Canterbury, from that holy see.
145 This, in our foresaid holy father's name,
    Pope Innocent, I do demand of thee.
  King John. What earthy name to interrogatories
    Can task the free breath of a sacred king?
    Thou canst not, cardinal, devise a name
150 So slight, unworthy and ridiculous,
    To charge me to an answer, as the Pope.
    Tell him this tale, and from the mouth of England
    Add thus much more, that no Italian priest
    Shall tithe or toll in our dominions,
155 But as we under heaven are supreme head,
    So under Him that great supremacy,
    Where we do reign, we will alone uphold,

142 *spurn* oppose with contempt *force perforce* by forcible means 147–48
What . . . king what mortal man can compel a king to answer questions
147 *interrogatories* formal questions put to a witness in a court of law
151 *charge* command 154 *tithe or toll* collect church revenues

Without th' assistance of a mortal hand.
So tell the Pope, all reverence set apart
To him and his usurped authority.   160
King Philip. Brother of England, you blaspheme in this.
King John. Though you and all the kings of Christendom
Are led so grossly by this meddling priest,
Dreading the curse that money may buy out,
And by the merit of vile gold, dross, dust,   165
Purchase corrupted pardon of a man,
Who in that sale sells pardon from himself,
Though you and all the rest, so grossly led,
This juggling witchcraft with revenue cherish,
Yet I alone, alone do me oppose   170
Against the Pope, and count his friends my foes.
Pandulph. Then, by the lawful power that I have,
Thou shalt stand cursed and excommunicate;
And blessèd shall he be that doth revolt
From his allegiance to an heretic;   175
And meritorious shall that hand be called,
Canonized and worshipped as a saint,
That takes away by any secret course
Thy hateful life.
Constance.   O lawful let it be
That I have room with Rome to curse awhile!   180
Good father cardinal, cry thou amen
To my keen curses, for without my wrong
There is no tongue hath power to curse him right.
Pandulph. There's law and warrant, lady, for my curse.
Constance. And for mine too. When law can do no right,   185
Let it be lawful that law bar no wrong.

159 *set apart* discarded 163 *grossly* stupidly 167 *Who ... himself* i.e. the
seller of indulgences damns his own soul 182–83 *without ... right* he
cannot be adequately cursed without recognition of his wrong against me

67

Law cannot give my child his kingdom here,
For he that holds his kingdom holds the law;
Therefore, since law itself is perfect wrong,
190   How can the law forbid my tongue to curse?
Pandulph. Philip of France, on peril of a curse,
Let go the hand of that arch-heretic,
And raise the power of France upon his head,
Unless he do submit himself to Rome.
195 *Elinor.* Look'st thou pale, France? Do not let go thy hand.
Constance. Look to that, devil, lest that France repent,
And by disjoining hands, hell lose a soul.
Austria. King Philip, listen to the cardinal.
Bastard. And hang a calfskin on his recreant limbs.
200 *Austria.* Well, ruffian, I must pocket up these wrongs,
  Because —
Bastard.   Your breeches best may carry them.
King John. Philip, what sayst thou to the cardinal?
Constance. What should he say, but as the cardinal?
Lewis. Bethink you, father, for the difference
205   Is purchase of a heavy curse from Rome,
Or the light loss of England for a friend.
Forgo the easier.
Blanch.   That's the curse of Rome.
Constance. O Lewis, stand fast! The devil tempts thee here
In likeness of a new untrimmèd bride.
210 *Blanch.* The Lady Constance speaks not from her faith,
  But from her need.
Constance.   O, if thou grant my need,
Which only lives but by the death of faith,

---

193 *upon* against   196 *devil* i.e. Elinor   200 *pocket up* put up with
207 *Forgo the easier* relinquish the less important   209 *new untrimmèd*
having just removed her bridal gown, still a virgin

That need must needs infer this principle,
That faith would live again by death of need.
O then, tread down my need, and faith mounts up;   215
Keep my need up, and faith is trodden down!
King John. The king is moved and answers not to this.
Constance. O be removed from him, and answer well!
Austria. Do so, King Philip; hang no more in doubt.
Bastard. Hang nothing but a calfskin, most sweet lout.   220
King Philip. I am perplexed, and know not what to say.
Pandulph. What canst thou say but will perplex thee more,
If thou stand excommunicate and cursed?
King Philip. Good reverend father, make my person yours,
And tell me how you would bestow yourself.   225
This royal hand and mine are newly knit,
And the conjunction of our inward souls
Married in league, coupled and linked together
With all religious strength of sacred vows.
The latest breath that gave the sound of words   230
Was deep-sworn faith, peace, amity, true love
Between our kingdoms and our royal selves,
And even before this truce, but new before,
No longer than we well could wash our hands
To clap this royal bargain up of peace,   235
Heaven knows, they were besmeared and overstained
With slaughter's pencil, where revenge did paint
The fearful difference of incensèd kings.
And shall these hands, so lately purged of blood,
So newly joined in love, so strong in both,   240

213 *needs* of necessity   224 *make my person yours* put yourself in my position   225 *bestow yourself* behave   230 *latest breath* most recent speech   235 *clap* strike the hands together to seal a bargain   238 *difference* quarrel

Unyoke this seizure and this kind regreet?
Play fast and loose with faith? So jest with heaven,
Make such unconstant children of ourselves,
As now again to snatch our palm from palm,
245 Unswear faith sworn, and on the marriage-bed
Of smiling peace to march a bloody host,
And make a riot on the gentle brow
Of true sincerity? O holy sir,
My reverend father, let it not be so!
250 Out of your grace, devise, ordain, impose
Some gentle order, and then we shall be blessed
To do your pleasure and continue friends.
Pandulph. All form is formless, order orderless,
Save what is opposite to England's love.
255 Therefore to arms! Be champion of our church,
Or let the church, our mother, breathe her curse,
A mother's curse, on her revolting son.
France, thou mayst hold a serpent by the tongue,
A casèd lion by the mortal paw,
260 A fasting tiger safer by the tooth,
Than keep in peace that hand which thou dost hold.
King Philip. I may disjoin my hand, but not my faith.
Pandulph. So mak'st thou faith an enemy to faith,
And like a civil war set'st oath to oath,
265 Thy tongue against thy tongue. O, let thy vow
First made to heaven, first be to heaven performed,
That is, to be the champion of our church.
What since thou swor'st is sworn against thyself
And may not be performèd by thyself,

241 *Unyoke this seizure* separate the hands clasped in friendship *regreet*
return of the salutation of friendship 242 *Play fast and loose* cheat
243 *unconstant* fickle 259 *casèd* caged *mortal* deadly 263–65 *So...
tongue* you are swearing against the religious faith to which you already
are pledged

For that which thou hast sworn to do amiss   270
Is not amiss when it is truly done;
And being not done, where doing tends to ill,
The truth is then most done not doing it.
The better act of purposes mistook
Is to mistake again; though indirect,   275
Yet indirection thereby grows direct,
And falsehood falsehood cures, as fire cools fire
Within the scorchèd veins of one new burned.
It is religion that doth make vows kept,
But thou hast sworn against religion,   280
By what thou swear'st, against the thing thou swear'st,
And mak'st an oath the surety for thy truth
Against an oath; the truth thou art unsure
To swear swears only not to be forsworn;
Else what a mockery should it be to swear!   285
But thou dost swear only to be forsworn;
And most forsworn to keep what thou dost swear.
Therefore thy later vows against thy first
Is in thyself rebellion to thyself,
And better conquest never canst thou make   290
Than arm thy constant and thy nobler parts
Against these giddy loose suggestions;
Upon which better part our prayers come in,
If thou vouchsafe them. But, if not, then know
The peril of our curses light on thee   295

270–78 *For ... burned* i.e. Philip by not performing what he has just vowed may turn his wrong to right; when one has done wrong it is often easier to return to the true path by another wrong than to retrace one's steps (this doctrine of equivocation was particularly hated by Elizabethan Protestants)   280–87 *But ... swear* since you have sworn by your faith against your faith (true religion), you make a mockery of swearing; you commit the greatest breach of faith by keeping the oath you have just sworn   291 *arm* by arming   292 *giddy* unsafe, insecure   *suggestions* temptations

So heavy as thou shalt not shake them off,
But in despair die under their black weight.
Austria. Rebellion, flat rebellion!
Bastard.   Will 't not be?
Will not a calfskin stop that mouth of thine?
Lewis. Father, to arms!
300 *Blanch.*   Upon thy wedding-day?
Against the blood that thou hast marrièd?
What, shall our feast be kept with slaughtered men?
Shall braying trumpets and loud churlish drums,
Clamors of hell, be measures to our pomp?
305 O husband, hear me! Ay, alack, how new
Is 'husband' in my mouth! Even for that name,
Which till this time my tongue did ne'er pronounce,
Upon my knee I beg, go not to arms
Against mine uncle.
Constance.   O, upon my knee,
310 Made hard with kneeling, I do pray to thee,
Thou virtuous Dauphin, alter not the doom
Forethought by heaven.
Blanch. Now shall I see thy love. What motive may
Be stronger with thee than the name of wife?
Constance. That which upholdeth him that thee up-
315   holds,
His honor. O thine honor, Lewis, thine honor!
Lewis. I muse your majesty doth seem so cold,
When such profound respects do pull you on.
Pandulph. I will denounce a curse upon his head.

296 *as* that   298 *Will 't not be* is nothing of any use   301 *blood* blood-
relationship   303 *churlish* rude   304 *measures* melodies   311 *doom* decision   312 *Forethought* predestined   318 *profound respects* weighty considerations   319 *denounce* proclaim

King Philip. Thou shalt not need. England, I will fall from
  thee.   320
Constance. O fair return of banished majesty!
Elinor. O foul revolt of French inconstancy!
King John. France, thou shalt rue this hour within this hour.
Bastard. Old time the clock-setter, that bald sexton time,
 Is it as he will? Well then, France shall rue.   325
Blanch. The sun's o'ercast with blood. Fair day, adieu!
 Which is the side that I must go withal?
 I am with both. Each army hath a hand,
 And in their rage, I having hold of both,
 They whirl asunder and dismember me.   330
 Husband, I cannot pray that thou mayst win.
 Uncle, I needs must pray that thou mayst lose.
 Father, I may not wish the fortune thine.
 Grandam, I will not wish thy wishes thrive.
 Whoever wins, on that side shall I lose;   335
 Assurèd loss before the match be played.
Lewis. Lady, with me, with me thy fortune lies.
Blanch. There where my fortune lives, there my life dies.
King John. Cousin, go draw our puissance together.
         [Exit Bastard.]
 France, I am burned up with inflaming wrath,   340
 A rage whose heat hath this condition,
 That nothing can allay, nothing but blood,
 The blood, and dearest-valued blood, of France.
King Philip. Thy rage shall burn thee up, and thou shalt
  turn

320 *fall from* forsake 324 *Old time the clock-setter* (the sexton's job included
setting the church clock as well as digging graves; he is thus easily iden-
tified with time, the destroyer of life) 339 *Cousin* kinsman *draw our
puissance* muster our army 341 *condition* quality

345 To ashes, ere our blood shall quench that fire.
  Look to thyself, thou art in jeopardy.
  King John. No more than he that threats. To arms let's hie
              Exeunt.

III, ii *Alarums, excursions. Enter Bastard, with Austria's head.*

  Bastard. Now, by my life, this day grows wondrous hot.
  Some airy devil hovers in the sky
  And pours down mischief. Austria's head lie there,
  While Philip breathes.

    Enter [King] John, Arthur, Hubert.

5 *King John.* Hubert, keep this boy. Philip, make up;
  My mother is assailèd in our tent,
  And ta'en, I fear.
  Bastard.   My lord, I rescued her;
  Her highness is in safety, fear you not.
  But on, my liege, for very little pains
10 Will bring this labor to a happy end.
         Exit [with the others].

III, iii *Alarums, excursions, retreat. Enter [King] John, Elinor,*
    Arthur, Bastard, Hubert, Lords.

  King John. [to Elinor] So shall it be; your grace shall stay
    behind
  So strongly guarded. *[to Arthur]* Cousin, look not sad.

III, ii, 2 *Some . . . sky* a thunderstorm threatens 4 *breathes* rests 5 *make
up* advance to the front line

74

Thy grandam loves thee, and thy uncle will
As dear be to thee as thy father was.

Arthur. O this will make my mother die with grief!   5

King John. [*to the Bastard*] Cousin, away for England! Haste
   before,
And ere our coming see thou shake the bags
Of hoarding abbots; imprisoned angels
Set at liberty. The fat ribs of peace
Must by the hungry now be fed upon.   10
Use our commission in his utmost force.

Bastard. Bell, book, and candle shall not drive me back
When gold and silver becks me to come on.
I leave your highness. Grandam, I will pray —
If ever I remember to be holy —   15
For your fair safety; so I kiss your hand.

Elinor. Farewell, gentle cousin.

King John.   Coz, farewell.   [*Exit Bastard.*]

Elinor. Come hither, little kinsman. Hark, a word.
                [*She takes Arthur aside.*]

King John. Come hither, Hubert. O my gentle Hubert,
We owe thee much! Within this wall of flesh   20
There is a soul counts thee her creditor,
And with advantage means to pay thy love;
And, my good friend, thy voluntary oath
Lives in this bosom, dearly cherishèd.
Give me thy hand. I had a thing to say,   25
But I will fit it with some better tune.
By heaven, Hubert, I am almost ashamed
To say what good respect I have of thee.

III, iii, 6 *before* ahead of us   8 *angels* coins (with the usual pun)   12 *Bell,
book, and candle* (instruments used in the ritual of excommunication)
13 *becks* beckons   17 *Coz* kinsman   22 *advantage* interest   *pay* repay
28 *respect* opinion

Hubert. I am much bounden to your majesty.

30 *King John.* Good friend, thou hast no cause to say so yet,
But thou shalt have; and creep time ne'er so slow,
Yet it shall come for me to do thee good.
I had a thing to say, but let it go.
The sun is in the heaven, and the proud day,

35 Attended with the pleasures of the world,
Is all too wanton and too full of gawds
To give me audience. If the midnight bell
Did with his iron tongue and brazen mouth
Sound on into the drowsy ear of night;

40 If this same were a churchyard where we stand,
And thou possessèd with a thousand wrongs;
Or if that surly spirit, melancholy,
Had baked thy blood and made it heavy, thick,
Which else runs tickling up and down the veins,

45 Making that idiot, laughter, keep men's eyes
And strain their cheeks to idle merriment,
A passion hateful to my purposes;
Or if that thou couldst see me without eyes,
Hear me without thine ears, and make reply

50 Without a tongue, using conceit alone,
Without eyes, ears, and harmful sound of words;
Then, in despite of brooded watchful day,
I would into thy bosom pour my thoughts.
But ah, I will not. Yet I love thee well,

55 And, by my troth, I think thou lov'st me well.
Hubert. So well, that what you bid me undertake,
Though that my death were adjunct to my act,
By heaven, I would do it.

---

29 *bounden* obliged 36 *gawds* showy ornaments, such as the flowers in
springtime 50 *conceit* understanding 52 *brooded* brooding 57 *adjunct
to* the result of

76

King John.   Do not I know thou wouldst?
Good Hubert! Hubert, Hubert, throw thine eye
On yon young boy. I'll tell thee what, my friend,   60
He is a very serpent in my way,
And wheresoe'er this foot of mine doth tread
He lies before me. Dost thou understand me?
Thou art his keeper.
Hubert.   And I'll keep him so
That he shall not offend your majesty.   65
King John. Death.
Hubert.   My lord?
King John.   A grave.
Hubert.   He shall not live.
King John.   Enough.
I could be merry now. Hubert, I love thee.
Well, I'll not say what I intend for thee.
Remember. Madam, fare you well.
I'll send those powers o'er to your majesty.   70
Elinor. My blessing go with thee!
King John.   For England, cousin, go.
Hubert shall be your man, attend on you
With all true duty. On toward Calais, ho!   *Exeunt.*

Enter [King Philip of] France, [Lewis, the] Dauphin,   III, iv
    Pandulph, Attendants.

King Philip. So, by a roaring tempest on the flood,
    A whole armado of convicted sail
    Is scattered and disjoined from fellowship.

70 *powers* troops   72 *man* servant   III, iv, 1 *flood* ocean   2 *armado* fleet
of warships   *convicted* doomed to destruction

Pandulph. Courage and comfort! All shall yet go well.
5 *King Philip.* What can go well when we have run so ill?
    Are we not beaten? Is not Angiers lost?
    Arthur ta'en prisoner? Divers dear friends slain?
    And bloody England into England gone,
    O'erbearing interruption, spite of France?
10 *Lewis.* What he hath won, that hath he fortified.
    So hot a speed with such advice disposed,
    Such temperate order in so fierce a cause,
    Doth want example. Who hath read or heard
    Of any kindred action like to this?
15 *King Philip.* Well could I bear that England had this praise,
    So we could find some pattern of our shame.

Enter Constance.

    Look, who comes here! A grave unto a soul,
    Holding th' eternal spirit, against her will,
    In the vile prison of afflicted breath.
20   I prithee, lady, go away with me.
Constance. Lo, now! Now see the issue of your peace!
King Philip. Patience, good lady! Comfort, gentle Constance!
Constance. No, I defy all counsel, all redress,
    But that which ends all counsel, true redress,
25   Death, death. O, amiable, lovely death!
    Thou odoriferous stench! Sound rottenness!
    Arise forth from the couch of lasting night,
    Thou hate and terror to prosperity,
    And I will kiss thy detestable bones,

9 *interruption* resistance *spite of* despite 11 *with such advice disposed*
controlled with such good judgment 13 *Doth want example* is without
precedent 16 *So* if *pattern* example in the past 19 *breath* life 23 *defy*
reject 27 *lasting* everlasting

And put my eyeballs in thy vaulty brows,   30
And ring these fingers with thy household worms,
And stop this gap of breath with fulsome dust,
And be a carrion monster like thyself.
Come, grin on me, and I will think thou smil'st
And buss thee as thy wife! Misery's love,   35
O, come to me!
King Philip.   O fair affliction, peace!
Constance. No, no, I will not, having breath to cry.
O that my tongue were in the thunder's mouth!
Then with a passion would I shake the world,
And rouse from sleep that fell anatomy   40
Which cannot hear a lady's feeble voice,
Which scorns a modern invocation.
Pandulph. Lady, you utter madness and not sorrow.
Constance. Thou art not holy to belie me so.
I am not mad; this hair I tear is mine.   45
My name is Constance; I was Geoffrey's wife.
Young Arthur is my son, and he is lost!
I am not mad. I would to heaven I were,
For then 'tis like I should forget myself.
O, if I could, what grief should I forget!   50
Preach some philosophy to make me mad,
And thou shalt be canonized, cardinal.
For, being not mad but sensible of grief,
My reasonable part produces reason
How I may be delivered of these woes,   55
And teaches me to kill or hang myself.
If I were mad, I should forget my son,

30 *vaulty* arched   32 *stop . . . breath* stop up this mouth   *fulsome* physi-
cally disgusting   35 *buss* kiss   40 *fell anatomy* cruel skeleton (as death
traditionally was personified)   42 *modern invocation* ordinary supplication
49 *like* probable   53 *sensible* capable   55 *be delivered of* give birth to, separate myself from (Constance sees death as her lover, grief as her child)

79

Or madly think a babe of clouts were he.
I am not mad. Too well, too well I feel
60   The different plague of each calamity.
King Philip. Bind up those tresses. O, what love I note
In the fair multitude of those her hairs!
Where but by chance a silver drop hath fallen,
Even to that drop ten thousand wiry friends
65   Do glue themselves in sociable grief,
Like true, inseparable, faithful loves,
Sticking together in calamity.
Constance. To England, if you will.
King Philip.   Bind up your hairs.
Constance. Yes, that I will; and wherefore will I do it?
70   I tore them from their bonds and cried aloud:
'O that these hands could so redeem my son,
As they have given these hairs their liberty!'
But now I envy at their liberty,
And will again commit them to their bonds,
75   Because my poor child is a prisoner.
And, Father Cardinal, I have heard you say
That we shall see and know our friends in heaven.
If that be true, I shall see my boy again,
For since the birth of Cain, the first male child,
80   To him that did but yesterday suspire,
There was not such a gracious creature born.
But now will canker sorrow eat my bud
And chase the native beauty from his cheek,

---

58 *babe of clouts* rag doll   63 *silver drop* tear   64 *wiry friends* hairs
(wire was a common metaphor for hair)   65 *sociable* sympathetic   68 *To England . . . will* (a line which is usually taken as evidence of some revision
in this scene, since it bears no relation to its immediate context, but
which may be an answer to King Philip's invitation at line 20)   81 *gracious*
meriting divine grace, destined for heaven   82 *canker* like a canker worm
(which destroys plants)

And he will look as hollow as a ghost,
As dim and meagre as an ague's fit,   85
And so he'll die; and rising so again,
When I shall meet him in the court of heaven
I shall not know him. Therefore never, never
Must I behold my pretty Arthur more.

Pandulph. You hold too heinous a respect of grief.   90

Constance. He talks to me that never had a son.

King Philip. You are as fond of grief as of your child.

Constance. Grief fills the room up of my absent child,
Lies in his bed, walks up and down with me,
Puts on his pretty looks, repeats his words,   95
Remembers me of all his gracious parts,
Stuffs out his vacant garments with his form.
Then have I reason to be fond of grief.
Fare you well. Had you such a loss as I,
I could give better comfort than you do.   100
I will not keep this form upon my head,
When there is such disorder in my wit.
O Lord! My boy, my Arthur, my fair son!
My life, my joy, my food, my all the world!
My widow-comfort, and my sorrows' cure!   *Exit.* 105

King Philip. I fear some outrage, and I'll follow her. *Exit.*

Lewis. There's nothing in this world can make me joy.
Life is as tedious as a twice-told tale,
Vexing the dull ear of a drowsy man,
And bitter shame hath spoiled the sweet world's taste,   110
That it yields nought but shame and bitterness.

Pandulph. Before the curing of a strong disease,
Even in the instant of repair and health,

---

85 *dim* pale 90 *heinous a respect* terrible an opinion 92 *fond of* foolishly infatuated with 96 *Remembers* reminds 101 *form* orderly arrangement of hair 102 *wit* mind 113 *repair* recovery

The fit is strongest. Evils that take leave,
115   On their departure most of all show evil.
What have you lost by losing of this day?
Lewis. All days of glory, joy, and happiness.
Pandulph. If you had won it, certainly you had.
No, no; when fortune means to men most good,
120   She looks upon them with a threat'ning eye.
'Tis strange to think how much King John hath lost
In this which he accounts so clearly won.
Are not you grieved that Arthur is his prisoner?
Lewis. As heartily as he is glad he hath him.
125 *Pandulph.* Your mind is all as youthful as your blood.
Now hear me speak with a prophetic spirit,
For even the breath of what I mean to speak
Shall blow each dust, each straw, each little rub,
Out of the path which shall directly lead
130   Thy foot to England's throne. And therefore mark:
John hath seized Arthur, and it cannot be
That, whiles warm life plays in that infant's veins,
The misplaced John should entertain an hour,
One minute, nay, one quiet breath of rest.
135   A sceptre snatched with an unruly hand
Must be as boisterously maintained as gained,
And he that stands upon a slippery place
Makes nice of no vile hold to stay him up.
That John may stand, then Arthur needs must fall;
140   So be it, for it cannot be but so.
Lewis. But what shall I gain by young Arthur's fall?
Pandulph. You, in the right of Lady Blanch your wife,
May then make all the claim that Arthur did.

116 *day* day of battle   128 *dust* grain of dust   *rub* obstacle (in the game
of bowls)   133 *misplaced* usurping   136 *boisterously* violently   138 *Makes*
... *up* is not scrupulous about what evil means he uses to support himself

Lewis. And lose it, life and all, as Arthur did.
Pandulph. How green you are and fresh in this old
    world! 145
  John lays you plots; the times conspire with you,
  For he that steeps his safety in true blood
  Shall find but bloody safety and untrue.
  This act so evilly borne shall cool the hearts
  Of all his people and freeze up their zeal, 150
  That none so small advantage shall step forth
  To check his reign, but they will cherish it;
  No natural exhalation in the sky,
  No scope of nature, no distempered day,
  No common wind, no customèd event, 155
  But they will pluck away his natural cause
  And call them meteors, prodigies, and signs,
  Abortives, presages, and tongues of heaven,
  Plainly denouncing vengeance upon John.
Lewis. May be he will not touch young Arthur's life, 160
  But hold himself safe in his prisonment.
Pandulph. O, sir, when he shall hear of your approach,
  If that young Arthur be not gone already,
  Even at that news he dies; and then the hearts
  Of all his people shall revolt from him 165
  And kiss the lips of unacquainted change,
  And pick strong matter of revolt and wrath
  Out of the bloody fingers' ends of John.

145 *green* inexperienced 146 *lays you plots* makes plans for your advantage
147–48 *he . . . untrue* he who bases his safety on his killing of the true king
(Arthur) will find his safety bloody and false 149 *so evilly borne* carried
out so wickedly 151 *advantage* opportunity 153 *exhalation* meteor
154 *scope of nature* a seemingly impossible event which is nevertheless within the possibility of nature *distempered* full of bad weather 155 *customèd*
ordinary 156 *his* its 158 *Abortives* corruptions of nature by untimely
birth 166 *kiss . . . change* be enamored of any new change 167–68 *pick
. . . John* find cause for revolt and anger in John's bloody deeds

Methinks I see this hurly all on foot;
170   And, O, what better matter breeds for you
Than I have named! The bastard Faulconbridge
Is now in England ransacking the church,
Offending charity. If but a dozen French
Were there in arms, they would be as a call
175   To train ten thousand English to their side,
Or as a little snow, tumbled about,
Anon becomes a mountain. O noble Dauphin,
Go with me to the king. 'Tis wonderful
What may be wrought out of their discontent,
180   Now that their souls are topful of offense.
For England go; I will whet on the king.
Lewis. Strong reasons make strange actions. Let us go.
If you say ay, the king will not say no.   *Exeunt.*

IV, i   *Enter Hubert and Executioners.*

Hubert. Heat me these irons hot, and look thou stand
Within the arras. When I strike my foot
Upon the bosom of the ground, rush forth
And bind the boy which you shall find with me
5   Fast to the chair. Be heedful. Hence, and watch.
[1.] Executioner. I hope your warrant will bear out the deed.

169 *hurly* commotion *on foot* started 170 *breeds* is ripening 173 *charity* good will 174 *call* decoy (as a bird call) 175 *train* attract 177 *Anon* soon 180 *topful of offense* filled to the brim with grievances 181 *whet on* incite IV, i, 2 *Within the arras* behind the curtains 3 *bosom* surface 6 *bear out* be sufficient to justify

Hubert. Uncleanly scruples! Fear not you. Look to 't.
                              [Exeunt Executioners.]
  Young lad, come forth; I have to say with you.

Enter Arthur.

Arthur. Good morrow, Hubert.
Hubert.   Good morrow, little prince.
Arthur. As little prince, having so great a title   10
  To be more prince, as may be. You are sad.
Hubert. Indeed, I have been merrier.
Arthur.   Mercy on me!
  Methinks nobody should be sad but I.
  Yet I remember, when I was in France
  Young gentlemen would be as sad as night,   15
  Only for wantonness. By my christendom,
  So I were out of prison and kept sheep,
  I should be as merry as the day is long;
  And so I would be here, but that I doubt
  My uncle practises more harm to me.   20
  He is afraid of me and I of him.
  Is it my fault that I was Geoffrey's son?
  No, indeed, is 't not, and I would to heaven
  I were your son, so you would love me, Hubert.
Hubert. *[aside]* If I talk to him, with his innocent prate   25
  He will awake my mercy which lies dead;
  Therefore I will be sudden and dispatch.

---

7 *Uncleanly* improper, unbecoming *Fear not you* don't you worry 8 *to
say with* something to say to 10–11 *As . . . may be* as little of a prince
(since I am in captivity) as one with my great title possibly could be
15–16 *as sad . . . wantonness* melancholy merely as a whimsical affectation
(a common pose among gentlemen of Shakespeare's day) 16 *christendom*
baptism, hence faith as a Christian 17 *So* if 19 *doubt* fear 20 *practises*
plots 25 *prate* prattle 27 *dispatch* do the job quickly

Arthur. Are you sick, Hubert? You look pale to-day.
 In sooth, I would you were a little sick,
30   That I might sit all night and watch with you.
 I warrant I love you more than you do me.
Hubert. [*aside*] His words do take possession of my bosom.
 Read here, young Arthur.   [*Shows a paper.*]
                    [*Aside*] How now, foolish rheum,
 Turning dispiteous torture out of door!
35   I must be brief, lest resolution drop
 Out at mine eyes in tender womanish tears.
 Can you not read it? Is it not fair writ?
Arthur. Too fairly, Hubert, for so foul effect.
 Must you with hot irons burn out both mine eyes?
Hubert. Young boy, I must.
Arthur.   And will you?
40 *Hubert.*   And I will.
Arthur. Have you the heart? When your head did but ache,
 I knit my handkercher about your brows –
 The best I had, a princess wrought it me –
 And I did never ask it you again;
45   And with my hand at midnight held your head,
 And like the watchful minutes to the hour,
 Still and anon cheered up the heavy time,
 Saying, 'What lack you?' and 'Where lies your grief?'
 Or 'What good love may I perform for you?'
50   Many a poor man's son would have lien still,
 And ne'er have spoke a loving word to you,

29 *sooth* truth 34 *dispiteous* merciless 37 *fair writ* clearly written
38 *effect* purpose 43 *wrought it me* embroidered it for me 46 *watchful
. . . hour* minutes which mark the progress of the hour 47 *Still and anon*
continually from time to time (Arthur compares his questions to the
ticking of the minutes, which makes the hour go by more quickly)
heavy dreary 49 *love* loving deed 50 *lien* lain (an archaic form pre-
served for the meter)

But you at your sick service had a prince.
Nay, you may think my love was crafty love,
And call it cunning; do and if you will.
If heaven be pleased that you must use me ill,   55
Why then you must. Will you put out mine eyes?
These eyes that never did nor never shall
So much as frown on you?
Hubert.   I have sworn to do it,
And with hot irons must I burn them out.
Arthur. Ah, none but in this iron age would do it!   60
The iron of itself, though heat red-hot,
Approaching near these eyes, would drink my tears
And quench this fiery indignation
Even in the matter of mine innocence,
Nay, after that, consume away in rust,   65
But for containing fire to harm mine eye.
Are you more stubborn-hard than hammered iron?
And if an angel should have come to me
And told me Hubert should put out mine eyes,
I would not have believed him – no tongue but Hubert's.   70
Hubert. [stamps] Come forth.

[Enter Executioners, with a cord, irons, etc.]

Do as I bid you do.
Arthur. O! save me, Hubert, save me! My eyes are out
Even with the fierce looks of these bloody men.
Hubert. Give me the iron, I say, and bind him here.   75
Arthur. Alas, what need you be so boist'rous rough?
I will not struggle, I will stand stone still.

52 *at your sick service* at your service (as a nurse) when you were sick
53 *crafty* pretended   60 *iron age* cruel, degenerate present (as opposed to
the heroic golden age of antiquity)   61 *heat* heated   64 *matter of mine
innocence* tears, the signs of innocence   66 *But* merely   76 *what* why

For heaven sake, Hubert, let me not be bound!
Nay, hear me, Hubert! Drive these men away,
80   And I will sit as quiet as a lamb.
I will not stir, nor wince, nor speak a word,
Nor look upon the iron angerly.
Thrust but these men away, and I'll forgive you,
Whatever torment you do put me to.
85 *Hubert.* Go, stand within. Let me alone with him.
   [1.] Executioner. I am best pleased to be from such a deed
                                                    [Exeunt Executioners.
   Arthur. Alas! I then have chid away my friend!
   He hath a stern look but a gentle heart.
   Let him come back, that his compassion may
   Give life to yours.
90 *Hubert.*   Come, boy, prepare yourself.
   Arthur. Is there no remedy?
   Hubert.   None, but to lose your eyes.
   Arthur. O heaven, that there were but a mote in yours,
   A grain, a dust, a gnat, a wandering hair,
   Any annoyance in that precious sense.
95   Then feeling what small things are boisterous there,
   Your vile intent must needs seem horrible.
   Hubert. Is this your promise? Go to, hold your tongue.
   Arthur. Hubert, the utterance of a brace of tongues
   Must needs want pleading for a pair of eyes.
100   Let me not hold my tongue, let me not, Hubert;
   Or, Hubert, if you will, cut out my tongue,
   So I may keep mine eyes. O, spare mine eyes,
   Though to no use but still to look on you!

82 *angerly* angrily   85 *Let . . . him* leave me to deal with him alone
86 *from* away from   87 *my friend* i.e. the executioner   92 *mote* speck of
dust   95 *boisterous* irritating   98–99 *the utterance . . . pleading* even two
tongues could not plead adequately

Lo, by my troth, the instrument is cold
And would not harm me.
Hubert.   I can heat it, boy.   105
Arthur. No, in good sooth. The fire is dead with grief,
    Being create for comfort, to be used
    In undeserved extremes. See else yourself.
    There is no malice in this burning coal.
    The breath of heaven hath blown his spirit out   110
    And strewed repentant ashes on his head.
Hubert. But with my breath I can revive it, boy.
Arthur. And if you do, you will but make it blush
    And glow with shame of your proceedings, Hubert.
    Nay, it perchance will sparkle in your eyes,   115
    And like a dog that is compelled to fight,
    Snatch at his master that doth tarre him on.
    All things that you should use to do me wrong
    Deny their office. Only you do lack
    That mercy which fierce fire and iron extends,   120
    Creatures of note for mercy-lacking uses.
Hubert. Well, see to live; I will not touch thine eye
    For all the treasure that thine uncle owes.
    Yet am I sworn and I did purpose, boy,
    With this same very iron to burn them out.   125
Arthur. O, now you look like Hubert! All this while
    You were disguisèd.
Hubert.   Peace! No more. Adieu.
    Your uncle must not know but you are dead.
    I'll fill these doggèd spies with false reports.

104 *troth* faith 107 *create* created 108 *In undeserved extremes* to inflict
acts of cruelty which have not been deserved 115 *sparkle* throw out sparks
117 *tarre* provoke to fight 119 *Deny their office* refuse to perform their
proper function 120 *extends* exhibit 121 *Creatures* i.e. fire and iron *of
note . . . uses* noted for their customary use in cruel affairs 123 *owes* owns
128 *but* other than that 129 *doggèd* malicious

130 And, pretty child, sleep doubtless and secure
       That Hubert for the wealth of all the world
       Will not offend thee.
    Arthur.   O heaven! I thank you, Hubert.
    Hubert. Silence! No more! Go closely in with me.
       Much danger do I undergo for thee.   *Exeunt*

IV, ii   *Enter [King] John, Pembroke, Salisbury, and other Lords.*

    King John. Here once again we sit, once again crowned,
       And looked upon, I hope, with cheerful eyes.
    Pembroke. This 'once again,' but that your highness pleased
       Was once superfluous. You were crowned before,
5   And that high royalty was ne'er plucked off,
       The faiths of men ne'er stainèd with revolt.
       Fresh expectation troubled not the land
       With any longed for change or better state.
    Salisbury. Therefore, to be possessed with double pomp,
10   To guard a title that was rich before,
       To gild refinèd gold, to paint the lily,
       To throw a perfume on the violet,
       To smooth the ice, or add another hue
       Unto the rainbow, or with taper-light
15   To seek the beauteous eye of heaven to garnish,
       Is wasteful and ridiculous excess.

130 *doubtless* without fear   *secure* assured   133 *closely* secretly   IV, ii,
once again (John has just had himself recrowned to mark the end of his dom-
ination by the church of Rome)   6 *stainèd* corrupted   7 *expectation* excited
anticipation of change   8 *state* government   9 *pomp* solemn ceremony (coronation)   10 *guard* ornament a garment with trimmings   14–15 *with taper-
light . . . garnish* to try to add to the sun's beauty by means of candlelight

Pembroke. But that your royal pleasure must be done,
 This act is as an ancient tale new told,
 And in the last repeating troublesome,
 Being urgèd at a time unseasonable. 20
Salisbury. In this the antique and well noted face
 Of plain old form is much disfigurèd,
 And like a shifted wind unto a sail,
 It makes the course of thoughts to fetch about,
 Startles and frights consideration, 25
 Makes sound opinion sick and truth suspected,
 For putting on so new a fashioned robe.
Pembroke. When workmen strive to do better than well,
 They do confound their skill in covetousness,
 And oftentimes excusing of a fault 30
 Doth make the fault the worse by the excuse,
 As patches set upon a little breach
 Discredit more in hiding of the fault
 Than did the fault before it was so patched.
Salisbury. To this effect, before you were new crowned, 35
 We breathed our counsel, but it pleased your highness
 To overbear it, and we are all well pleased,
 Since all and every part of what we would
 Doth make a stand at what your highness will.
King John. Some reasons of this double coronation 40
 I have possessed you with and think them strong;
 And more, more strong, when lesser is my fear,

22 *plain old form* simple customary behavior   23 *shifted wind* change of wind
24 *fetch about* change their direction   25 *consideration* thought (about the
succession; by a second coronation John is causing others to question the
validity of his title)   29 *confound . . . covetousness* destroy what they
have done well by their desire to do even better   32 *breach* hole in a garment   33 *fault* defect   36 *breathed* spoke   37 *overbear* veto by superior
power   38–39 *Since . . . will* since our wishes can never run counter to
your desires   41 *possessed you with* informed you of

I shall indue you with. Meantime but ask
What you would have reformed that is not well,
45   And well shall you perceive how willingly
I will both hear and grant you your requests.
Pembroke. Then I, as one that am the tongue of
    these
To sound the purposes of all their hearts,
Both for myself and them – but, chief of all,
50   Your safety, for the which myself and them
Bend their best studies – heartily request
Th' enfranchisement of Arthur, whose restraint
Doth move the murmuring lips of discontent
To break into this dangerous argument:
55   If what in rest you have in right you hold,
Why then your fears, which, as they say, attend
The steps of wrong, should move you to mew up
Your tender kinsman, and to choke his days
With barbarous ignorance and deny his youth
60   The rich advantage of good exercise.
That the time's enemies may not have this
To grace occasions, let it be our suit
That you have bid us ask, his liberty,
Which for our goods we do no further ask
65   Than whereupon our weal, on you depending,
Counts it your weal he have his liberty.

43 *indue* furnish   48 *sound the purposes* express the proposals   50 *them*
they   51 *Bend their best studies* direct their most diligent efforts   52 *enfranchisement* release from prison   55 *If . . . hold* if you hold right-
fully what you possess peaceably   57 *mew up* shut up   60 *exercise* education of a gentleman   61 *time's enemies* those opposed to the present state
of affairs   62 *grace occasions* make proper and acceptable their opportuni-
ties to attack   64 *our goods* our own good   65 *whereupon* to the extent
that   *weal* welfare

Enter Hubert.

King John. Let it be so. I do commit his youth
   To your direction. Hubert, what news with you?
                           [Takes him apart.]
Pembroke. This is the man should do the bloody deed;
   He showed his warrant to a friend of mine.   70
   The image of a wicked heinous fault
   Lives in his eye. That close aspect of his
   Does show the mood of a much troubled breast,
   And I do fearfully believe 'tis done,
   What we so feared he had a charge to do.   75
Salisbury. The color of the king doth come and go
   Between his purpose and his conscience,
   Like heralds 'twixt two dreadful battles set.
   His passion is so ripe it needs must break.
Pembroke. And when it breaks, I fear will issue thence   80
   The foul corruption of a sweet child's death.
King John. We cannot hold mortality's strong hand.
   Good lords, although my will to give is living,
   The suit which you demand is gone and dead.
   He tells us Arthur is deceased to-night.   85
Salisbury. Indeed we feared his sickness was past cure.
Pembroke. Indeed we heard how near his death he was,
   Before the child himself felt he was sick.
   This must be answered either here or hence.
King John. Why do you bend such solemn brows
   on me?   90

71 *image* reflection   72 *close aspect* secret expression   75 *charge* order
78 *battles* armies arranged for battle   *set* assigned to perform duties
79 *break* burst open (like a boil)   81 *corruption* pus   89 *answered* accounted or atoned for   *here or hence* in this world or the next   90 *bend . . .*
brows frown

Think you I bear the shears of destiny?
Have I commandment on the pulse of life?
Salisbury. It is apparent foul play, and 'tis shame
That greatness should so grossly offer it.
95 So thrive it in your game! And so, farewell.
Pembroke. Stay yet, Lord Salisbury. I'll go with thee
And find th' inheritance of this poor child,
His little kingdom of a forcèd grave.
That blood which owed the breadth of all this isle,
100 Three foot of it doth hold — bad world the while!
This must not be thus borne. This will break out
To all our sorrows, and ere long, I doubt.

Exeunt [Lords].

King John. They burn in indignation. I repent.

Enter Messenger.

There is no sure foundation set on blood,
105 No certain life achieved by others' death.
A fearful eye thou hast. Where is that blood
That I have seen inhabit in those cheeks?
So foul a sky clears not without a storm.
Pour down thy weather. How goes all in France?
110 *Messenger.* From France to England. Never such a power
For any foreign preparation
Was levied in the body of a land.
The copy of your speed is learned by them,

---

91 *shears of destiny* instrument with which Atropos, one of the three
Fates, cuts the thread of life   94 *That ... offer it* that a king should act
so outrageously   95 *So ... game* may you suffer accordingly   98 *forcèd*
imposed by violence   99 *blood* life   *owed* owned   100 *the while* where
such things can happen   101 *borne* tolerated   102 *doubt* fear   106 *fearful*
full of fear   109 *weather* tempest   111 *preparation* expedition   113 *copy*
example   *learned* imitated

For when you should be told they do prepare,
The tidings comes that they are all arrived.   115
King John. O, where hath our intelligence been drunk?
  Where hath it slept? Where is my mother's care,
  That such an army could be drawn in France,
  And she not hear of it?
Messenger.   My liege, her ear
  Is stopped with dust. The first of April died   120
  Your noble mother; and, as I hear, my lord,
  The Lady Constance in a frenzy died
  Three days before. But this from rumor's tongue
  I idly heard; if true or false I know not.
King John. Withhold thy speed, dreadful occasion!   125
  O, make a league with me, till I have pleased
  My discontented peers. What! Mother dead!
  How wildly then walks my estate in France!
  Under whose conduct came those powers of France
  That thou for truth giv'st out are landed here?   130
Messenger. Under the Dauphin.
King John.   Thou hast made me giddy
  With these ill tidings.

          Enter Bastard and Peter of Pomfret.

                Now, what says the world
  To your proceedings? Do not seek to stuff
  My head with more ill news, for it is full.

115 *arrived* landed   116 *intelligence* spy system   118 *drawn* mustered
119–23 *her ear . . . before* (Queen Elinor actually died on April 1, 1204,
but how Shakespeare could have gotten the day and month exactly right
remains a mystery, for this was not recorded in any Elizabethan chronicle.
Constance had died three years before, in 1201. Shakespeare compresses
time.)   124 *idly* without paying full attention   125 *occasion* course of
events   128 *walks* proceeds   *estate* power   129 *conduct* leadership

135 *Bastard.* But if you be afeard to hear the worst,
  Then let the worst unheard fall on your head.
  King John. Bear with me, cousin, for I was amazed
   Under the tide; but now I breathe again
   Aloft the flood and can give audience
140   To any tongue, speak it of what it will.
  Bastard. How I have sped among the clergymen
   The sums I have collected shall express.
   But as I travelled hither through the land,
   I find the people strangely fantasied,
145   Possessed with rumors, full of idle dreams,
   Not knowing what they fear, but full of fear.
   And here's a prophet that I brought with me
   From forth the streets of Pomfret, whom I found
   With many hundreds treading on his heels,
150   To whom he sung, in rude harsh-sounding rimes,
   That ere the next Ascension-day at noon,
   Your highness should deliver up your crown.
  King John. Thou idle dreamer, wherefore didst thou so?
  Peter. Foreknowing that the truth will fall out so.
155 *King John.* Hubert, away with him; imprison him,
   And on that day at noon, whereon he says
   I shall yield up my crown, let him be hanged.
   Deliver him to safety and return,
   For I must use thee.   *[Exit Hubert, with Peter.]*
     O my gentle cousin,
160   Hear'st thou the news abroad, who are arrived?
  Bastard. The French, my lord. Men's mouths are full of it.
   Besides, I met Lord Bigot and Lord Salisbury,
   With eyes as red as new-enkindled fire,

137 *amazed* bewildered   139 *Aloft* above   141 *sped* succeeded   144 *strangely
fantasied* full of strange notions   148 *Pomfret* Pontefract in Yorkshire
153 *idle* foolish   158 *safety* safekeeping   159 *gentle* noble

And others more, going to seek the grave
Of Arthur, whom they say is killed to-night   165
On your suggestion.
King John.   Gentle kinsman, go,
And thrust thyself into their companies.
I have a way to win their loves again.
Bring them before me.
Bastard.   I will seek them out.
King John. Nay, but make haste, the better foot before.   170
O, let me have no subject enemies,
When adverse foreigners affright my towns
With dreadful pomp of stout invasion.
Be Mercury, set feathers to thy heels,
And fly like thought from them to me again.   175
Bastard. The spirit of the time shall teach me speed.   *Exit.*
King John. Spoke like a sprightful noble gentleman.
Go after him, for he perhaps shall need
Some messenger betwixt me and the peers;
And be thou he.
Messenger.   With all my heart, my liege.   *[Exit.]* 180
King John. My mother dead!

Enter Hubert.

Hubert. My lord, they say five moons were seen to-night –
Four fixèd, and the fifth did whirl about
The other four in wondrous motion.
King John. Five moons!
Hubert.   Old men and beldams in the streets 185
Do prophesy upon it dangerously.

167 *thrust . . . companies* associate with them   172 *adverse* hostile   173 *stout*
bold   174 *Mercury* the messenger of the gods, who wore winged sandals
177 *sprightful* full of spirit   182 *five moons* (a type of unnatural phenomenon believed to herald disaster to a kingdom)   185 *beldams* hags   186 *prophesy upon it* attempt to explain the unnatural phenomenon

Young Arthur's death is common in their mouths,
And when they talk of him, they shake their heads
And whisper one another in the ear;
190 And he that speaks doth gripe the hearer's wrist,
Whilst he that hears makes fearful action,
With wrinkled brows, with nods, with rolling eyes.
I saw a smith stand with his hammer, thus,
The whilst his iron did on the anvil cool,
195 With open mouth swallowing a tailor's news;
Who, with his shears and measure in his hand,
Standing on slippers, which his nimble haste
Had falsely thrust upon contrary feet,
Told of a many thousand warlike French,
200 That were embattailèd and ranked in Kent.
Another lean unwashed artificer
Cuts off his tale and talks of Arthur's death.
King John. Why seek'st thou to possess me with these fears?
Why urgest thou so oft young Arthur's death?
205 Thy hand hath murdered him. I had a mighty cause
To wish him dead, but thou hadst none to kill him.
Hubert. No had, my lord? Why, did you not provoke me?
King John. It is the curse of kings to be attended
By slaves that take their humors for a warrant
210 To break within the bloody house of life,
And on the winking of authority
To understand a law, to know the meaning
Of dangerous majesty, when, perchance, it frowns
More upon humor than advised respect.

191 *action* gesticulation 198 *contrary* wrong 200 *embattailèd and ranked* ready for battle and arrayed in proper order 207 *No had* had I not *provoke* incite 208 *attended* served 209 *humors* whims 210 *bloody house of life* human body, containing blood 211 *winking of authority* failure of the king to enforce the law 212 *understand* infer 214 *upon humor* because of a whim *advised respect* carefully considered decision

Hubert. Here is your hand and seal for what I did.   215
King John. O, when the last accompt 'twixt heaven and
      earth
   Is to be made, then shall this hand and seal
   Witness against us to damnation!
   How oft the sight of means to do ill deeds
   Makes deeds ill done! Hadst not thou been by,   220
   A fellow by the hand of nature marked,
   Quoted and signed to do a deed of shame,
   This murder had not come into my mind;
   But taking note of thy abhorred aspect,
   Finding thee fit for bloody villainy,   225
   Apt, liable to be employed in danger,
   I faintly broke with thee of Arthur's death;
   And thou, to be endearèd to a king,
   Made it no conscience to destroy a prince.
Hubert. My lord —   230
King John. Hadst thou but shook thy head or made a pause
   When I spake darkly what I purposèd,
   Or turned an eye of doubt upon my face,
   As bid me tell my tale in express words,
   Deep shame had struck me dumb, made me break off,   235
   And those thy fears might have wrought fears in me.
   But thou didst understand me by my signs
   And didst in signs again parley with sin;
   Yea, without stop, didst let thy heart consent,
   And consequently thy rude hand to act   240
   The deed which both our tongues held vile to name.
   Out of my sight, and never see me more!

216 *accompt* account, judgment   222 *Quoted and signed* especially noted and
marked out   224 *abhorred aspect* horrible appearance   226 *liable* suitable
227 *faintly broke with* hesitatingly confided in   229 *conscience* matter of
conscience   232 *darkly* vaguely   234 *As* as if to   *in express words* clearly

My nobles leave me, and my state is braved,
Even at my gates, with ranks of foreign powers.
245 Nay, in the body of this fleshly land,
This kingdom, this confine of blood and breath,
Hostility and civil tumult reigns
Between my conscience and my cousin's death.

Hubert. Arm you against your other enemies;
250 I'll make a peace between your soul and you.
Young Arthur is alive. This hand of mine
Is yet a maiden and an innocent hand,
Not painted with the crimson spots of blood.
Within this bosom never entered yet
255 The dreadful motion of a murderous thought,
And you have slandered nature in my form,
Which, howsoever rude exteriorly,
Is yet the cover of a fairer mind
Than to be butcher of an innocent child.

King John. Doth Arthur live? O, haste thee to the
260   peers!
Throw this report on their incensèd rage,
And make them tame to their obedience.
Forgive the comment that my passion made
Upon thy feature, for my rage was blind,
265 And foul imaginary eyes of blood
Presented thee more hideous than thou art.
O, answer not, but to my closet bring

---

243 *braved* defied   245 *fleshly land* his human body (conceived of as a
little world paralleling the physical universe in its composition)   246 *confine* territory bound by frontiers   247 *civil tumult* internal war   252 *maiden*
bloodless   255 *motion* impulse   256 *form* outward appearance   261 *Throw*
i.e. as water, to quench the fire of rage   264 *feature* appearance   265 *imaginary eyes of blood* i.e. Hubert's eyes, which in John's imagination
seemed full of blood   267 *closet* private room

The angry lords with all expedient haste.
I conjure thee but slowly; run more fast.   *Exeunt.*

Enter Arthur, on the walls.   IV, iii

Arthur. The wall is high, and yet will I leap down.
  Good ground, be pitiful and hurt me not!
  There's few or none do know me; if they did,
  This ship-boy's semblance hath disguised me quite.
  I am afraid, and yet I'll venture it.   5
  If I get down, and do not break my limbs,
  I'll find a thousand shifts to get away.
  As good to die and go, as die and stay.   *[Leaps down.]*
  O me! My uncle's spirit is in these stones!
  Heaven take my soul, and England keep my bones!   10
                                                    Dies.

Enter Pembroke, Salisbury, and Bigot.

Salisbury. Lords, I will meet him at Saint Edmundsbury.
  It is our safety, and we must embrace
  This gentle offer of the perilous time.
Pembroke. Who brought that letter from the cardinal?
Salisbury. The Count Melun, a noble lord of France,   15
  Whose private with me of the Dauphin's love
  Is much more general than these lines import.
Bigot. To-morrow morning let us meet him then.

269 *conjure* solemnly urge IV, iii, 4 *semblance* disguise 7 *shifts* strata-
gems 11 *him* i.e. the Dauphin 12 *embrace* welcome 16 *private* private
communication *love* friendship 17 *general* comprehensive

Salisbury. Or rather then set forward, for 'twill be
20　Two long days' journey, lords, or ere we meet.

Enter Bastard.

Bastard. Once more to-day well met, distempered lords!
　　The king by me requests your presence straight.
Salisbury. The king hath dispossessed himself of us.
　　We will not line his thin bestainèd cloak
25　With our pure honors, nor attend the foot
　　That leaves the print of blood where'er it walks.
　　Return and tell him so. We know the worst.
Bastard. Whate'er you think, good words, I think, were
　　best.
Salisbury. Our griefs, and not our manners, reason now.
30 *Bastard.* But there is little reason in your grief;
　　Therefore 'twere reason you had manners now.
Pembroke. Sir, sir, impatience hath his privilege.
Bastard. 'Tis true, to hurt his master, no man else.
Salisbury. This is the prison. *[Sees Arthur.]* What is he lies
　　here?
Pembroke. O death, made proud with pure and princely
35　beauty!
　　The earth had not a hole to hide this deed.
Salisbury. Murder, as hating what himself hath done,
　　Doth lay it open to urge on revenge.
Bigot. Or when he doomed this beauty to a grave,
40　Found it too precious princely for a grave.
Salisbury. Sir Richard, what think you? Have you beheld,
　　Or have you read or heard, or could you think,

20 *or ere* before　21 *distempered* disgruntled　22 *straight* at once　29 *griefs*
grievances　*reason* talk　40 *too . . . grave* (bodies of princes were en-
tombed above ground)

Or do you almost think, although you see,
That you do see? Could thought, without this object,
Form such another? This is the very top,   45
The height, the crest, or crest unto the crest,
Of murder's arms. This is the bloodiest shame,
The wildest savagery, the vilest stroke,
That ever wall-eyed wrath or staring rage
Presented to the tears of soft remorse.   50

Pembroke. All murders past do stand excused in this.
And this, so sole and so unmatchable,
Shall give a holiness, a purity,
To the yet unbegotten sin of times,
And prove a deadly bloodshed but a jest,   55
Exampled by this heinous spectacle.

Bastard. It is a damnèd and a bloody work,
The graceless action of a heavy hand,
If that it be the work of any hand.

Salisbury. If that it be the work of any hand!   60
We had a kind of light what would ensue.
It is the shameful work of Hubert's hand,
The practice and the purpose of the king,
From whose obedience I forbid my soul,
Kneeling before this ruin of sweet life,   65
And breathing to his breathless excellence
The incense of a vow, a holy vow,
Never to taste the pleasures of the world,
Never to be infected with delight,
Nor conversant with ease and idleness,   70

44 *That* that which   49 *wall-eyed* with glaring eyes   *rage* madness   50 *re-morse* pity   52 *sole* unique   54 *times* future ages   56 *Exampled by* com-pared with   58 *graceless* unholy   *heavy* wicked   61 *light* inkling   63 *prac-tice* machination   69 *infected* diseased (delight under such circumstances is conceived of as a disease)

Till I have set a glory to this hand,
By giving it the worship of revenge.

Pembroke.   }
Bigot.   } Our souls religiously confirm thy words.

Enter Hubert.

Hubert. Lords, I am hot with haste in seeking you.
75   Arthur doth live; the king hath sent for you.
Salisbury. O, he is bold and blushes not at death.
     Avaunt, thou hateful villain! Get thee gone!
Hubert. I am no villain.
Salisbury.   *[drawing his sword]* Must I rob the law?
Bastard. Your sword is bright, sir; put it up again.
80 *Salisbury.* Not till I sheathe it in a murderer's skin.
Hubert. Stand back, Lord Salisbury, stand back, I say!
     By heaven, I think my sword's as sharp as yours.
     I would not have you, lord, forget yourself,
     Nor tempt the danger of my true defense,
85   Lest I, by marking of your rage, forget
     Your worth, your greatness, and nobility.
Bigot. Out, dunghill! Dar'st thou brave a nobleman?
Hubert. Not for my life, but yet I dare defend
     My innocent life against an emperor.
Salisbury. Thou art a murderer.
90 *Hubert.*   Do not prove me so.
     Yet I am none. Whose tongue soe'er speaks false,
     Not truly speaks; who speaks not truly, lies.
Pembroke. Cut him to pieces.
Bastard.   Keep the peace, I say.

71 *this hand* i.e. either the dead Arthur's hand which Salisbury kisses, or
his own hand raised in celebration of his vow   72 *worship* honor, dignity
77 *Avaunt* be gone   84 *true defense* (1) honest defense of my cause (2)
skilful use of my sword   85 *marking of* (1) observing (2) striking a blow
at   87 *brave* insult   90 *Do . . . so* i.e. by compelling me to kill you

Salisbury. Stand by, or I shall gall you, Faulconbridge.
Bastard. Thou wert better gall the devil, Salisbury.   95
  If thou but frown on me, or stir thy foot,
  Or teach thy hasty spleen to do me shame,
  I'll strike thee dead. Put up thy sword betime,
  Or I'll so maul you and your toasting-iron
  That you shall think the devil is come from hell.   100
Bigot. What wilt thou do, renownèd Faulconbridge?
  Second a villain and a murderer?
Hubert. Lord Bigot, I am none.
Bigot.   Who killed this prince?
Hubert. 'Tis not an hour since I left him well.
  I honored him, I loved him, and will weep   105
  My date of life out for his sweet life's loss.
Salisbury. Trust not those cunning waters of his eyes,
  For villainy is not without such rheum,
  And he, long traded in it, makes it seem
  Like rivers of remorse and innocency.   110
  Away with me, all you whose souls abhor
  Th' uncleanly savors of a slaughter-house,
  For I am stifled with this smell of sin.
Bigot. Away toward Bury, to the Dauphin there!
Pembroke. There tell the king he may inquire us out.   115
                                    Exeunt Lords.
Bastard. Here's a good world! Knew you of this fair work?
  Beyond the infinite and boundless reach
  Of mercy, if thou didst this deed of death,
  Art thou damned, Hubert.
Hubert.   Do but hear me, sir.
Bastard. Ha! I'll tell thee what.   120

94 *by* aside *gall* injure 97 *spleen* wrath 98 *betime* at once 99 *toasting-iron* sword (a term of contempt) 102 *Second* support 106 *date* duration 109 *long traded* experienced 112 *savors* odors

Thou'rt damned as black – nay, nothing is so black.
Thou art more deep damned than Prince Lucifer.
There is not yet so ugly a fiend of hell
As thou shalt be, if thou didst kill this child.

Hubert. Upon my soul –

125 *Bastard.* If thou didst but consent
To this most cruel act, do but despair,
And if thou want'st a cord, the smallest thread
That ever spider twisted from her womb
Will serve to strangle thee; a rush will be a beam
130 To hang thee on. Or wouldst thou drown thyself,
Put but a little water in a spoon,
And it shall be as all the ocean,
Enough to stifle such a villain up.
I do suspect thee very grievously.

135 *Hubert.* If I in act, consent, or sin of thought,
Be guilty of the stealing that sweet breath
Which was embounded in this beauteous clay,
Let hell want pains enough to torture me.
I left him well.

Bastard. Go, bear him in thine arms.
140 I am amazed, methinks, and lose my way
Among the thorns and dangers of this world.
How easy dost thou take all England up!
From forth this morsel of dead royalty
The life, the right and truth of all this realm
145 Is fled to heaven, and England now is left
To tug and scamble and to part by th' teeth
The unowed interest of proud swelling state.

121 *black* (the traditional color of the devil and of all damned souls)
129 *rush* slender reed 137 *embounded . . . clay* enclosed within this beautiful body 140 *amazed* bewildered 146 *scamble* scramble 147 *unowed interest* disputed ownership

Now for the bare-picked bone of majesty
Doth doggèd war bristle his angry crest
And snarleth in the gentle eyes of peace.   150
Now powers from home and discontents at home
Meet in one line, and vast confusion waits,
As doth a raven on a sick-fallen beast,
The imminent decay of wrested pomp.
Now happy he whose cloak and ceinture can   155
Hold out this tempest. Bear away that child,
And follow me with speed. I'll to the king.
A thousand businesses are brief in hand,
And heaven itself doth frown upon the land.   *Exit.*

Enter King John and Pandulph [with] Attendants.   V, i

King John. Thus have I yielded up into your hand
  The circle of my glory.
Pandulph.   *[giving King John the crown]* Take again
  From this my hand, as holding of the Pope,
  Your sovereign greatness and authority.
King John. Now keep your holy word. Go meet the French, 5
  And from his holiness use all your power
  To stop their marches 'fore we are enflamed.
  Our discontented counties do revolt.
  Our people quarrel with obedience,
  Swearing allegiance and the love of soul   10

149 *doggèd* (1) fierce (2) like a dog **151** *from home* foreign *discontents*
rebels **152** *in one line* together **154** *wrested pomp* usurped kingship
155 *ceinture* belt **158** *brief in hand* calling for immediate attention
V, i, **2** *circle* crown **8** *counties* shires, or noblemen **10** *love of soul* deep-
est love, loyalty

To stranger blood, to foreign royalty.
This inundation of mistempered humor
Rests by you only to be qualified.
Then pause not, for the present time's so sick,
15   That present med'cine must be ministered,
Or overthrow incurable ensues.
    Pandulph. It was my breath that blew this tempest up,
Upon your stubborn usage of the Pope,
But since you are a gentle convertite,
20   My tongue shall hush again this storm of war
And make fair weather in your blust'ring land.
On this Ascension-day, remember well,
Upon your oath of service to the Pope,
Go I to make the French lay down their arms.   *Exit.*
25 *King John.* Is this Ascension-day? Did not the prophet
Say that before Ascension-day at noon
My crown I should give off? Even so I have.
I did suppose it should be on constraint,
But, heaven be thanked, it is but voluntary.

Enter Bastard.

30 *Bastard.* All Kent hath yielded; nothing there holds out
But Dover Castle. London hath received,
Like a kind host, the Dauphin and his powers.
Your nobles will not hear you, but are gone
To offer service to your enemy,
35   And wild amazement hurries up and down
The little number of your doubtful friends.

---

12 *inundation . . . humor* overgrowth, because of disorder, of one of the
four elements of the body (John is drawing his metaphor from current med-
ical terminology)   13 *Rests . . . qualified* can be reduced to proper propor-
tions only by you   15 *ministered* administered   16 *overthrow* destruction
18 *Upon* because of   19 *convertite* convert   27 *give off* relinquish   35 *amazement* bewilderment   36 *doubtful* (1) frightened (2) of questionable loyalty

King John. Would not my lords return to me again
  After they heard young Arthur was alive?
Bastard. They found him dead and cast into the streets,
  An empty casket, where the jewel of life   40
  By some damned hand was robbed and ta'en away.
King John. That villain Hubert told me he did live.
Bastard. So, on my soul, he did, for aught he knew.
  But wherefore do you droop? Why look you sad?
  Be great in act, as you have been in thought.   45
  Let not the world see fear and sad distrust
  Govern the motion of a kingly eye.
  Be stirring as the time; be fire with fire.
  Threaten the threat'ner, and outface the brow
  Of bragging horror. So shall inferior eyes,   50
  That borrow their behaviors from the great,
  Grow great by your example and put on
  The dauntless spirit of resolution.
  Away, and glister like the god of war
  When he intendeth to become the field.   55
  Show boldness and aspiring confidence.
  What, shall they seek the lion in his den
  And fright him there? And make him tremble
    there?
  O, let it not be said! Forage, and run
  To meet displeasure farther from the doors,   60
  And grapple with him ere he come so nigh.
King John. The legate of the Pope hath been with me,
  And I have made a happy peace with him,
  And he hath promised to dismiss the powers
  Led by the Dauphin.
Bastard.   O inglorious league!   65

---

48 *stirring* energetic 49 *outface* stare down 54 *glister* shine in armor
55 *become* adorn 59 *Forage* seek out the enemy 63 *happy* favorable

Shall we, upon the footing of our land,
Send fair-play orders and make compromise,
Insinuation, parley, and base truce
To arms invasive? Shall a beardless boy,
70 A cockered silken wanton, brave our fields
And flesh his spirit in a warlike soil,
Mocking the air with colors idly spread,
And find no check? Let us, my liege, to arms!
Perchance the cardinal cannot make your peace;
75 Or if he do, let it at least be said
They saw we had a purpose of defense.
King John. Have thou the ordering of this present time.
Bastard. Away then, with good courage! Yet, I know,
Our party may well meet a prouder foe.   *Exeunt.*

V, ii   *Enter (in arms) [Lewis, the] Dauphin, Salisbury, Melun,*
           Pembroke, Bigot, Soldiers.

Lewis. My Lord Melun, let this be copied out,
And keep it safe for our remembrance.
Return the precedent to those lords again,
That, having our fair order written down,
5 Both they and we, perusing o'er these notes,
May know wherefore we took the sacrament,
And keep our faiths firm and inviolable.

66 *upon . . . land* standing on our native ground   67 *fair-play orders* chiv-
alric stipulations   68 *Insinuation* self-ingratiation   69 *invasive* invading
70 *cockered* pampered   *wanton* spoilt child   *brave* (1) insult (2) display
his finery in   71 *flesh* initiate in bloodshed   72 *idly* carelessly   73 *check*
resistance   79 *prouder* more powerful   V, ii, 3 *precedent* first draft of
treaty   4 *fair order* equitable conditions

Salisbury. Upon our sides it never shall be broken.
　　And, noble Dauphin, albeit we swear
　　A voluntary zeal and an unurgèd faith   10
　　To your proceedings, yet believe me, prince,
　　I am not glad that such a sore of time
　　Should seek a plaster by contemnèd revolt,
　　And heal the inveterate canker of one wound
　　By making many. O, it grieves my soul   15
　　That I must draw this metal from my side
　　To be a widow-maker! O, and there
　　Where honorable rescue and defense
　　Cries out upon the name of Salisbury.
　　But such is the infection of the time   20
　　That, for the health and physic of our right,
　　We cannot deal but with the very hand
　　Of stern injustice and confusèd wrong.
　　And is 't not pity, O my grievèd friends,
　　That we, the sons and children of this isle,   25
　　Were born to see so sad an hour as this,
　　Wherein we step after a stranger, march
　　Upon her gentle bosom, and fill up
　　Her enemies' ranks — I must withdraw and weep
　　Upon the spot of this enforcèd cause —   30
　　To grace the gentry of a land remote,
　　And follow unacquainted colors here?
　　What, here? O nation, that thou couldst remove!
　　That Neptune's arms, who clippeth thee about,
　　Would bear thee from the knowledge of thyself,   35

10 *unurgèd* uncompelled 13 *plaster* dressing for a wound *contemned* de-
spised 14 *inveterate canker* chronic sore 16 *metal* sword 19 *Cries out
upon* appeals to 21 *physic* cure 22 *deal* act 30 *spot* disgrace *enforcèd*
forced upon us 31 *grace* pay homage to 32 *unacquainted colors* foreign
banners 33 *remove* move yourself, depart 34 *clippeth* embraces
35 *knowledge* awareness

And grapple thee unto a pagan shore,
Where these two Christian armies might combine
The blood of malice in a vein of league,
And not to spend it so unneighborly!

40 *Lewis.* A noble temper dost thou show in this,
And great affections wrestling in thy bosom
Doth make an earthquake of nobility.
O, what a noble combat hast thou fought
Between compulsion and a brave respect!

45 Let me wipe off this honorable dew,
That silverly doth progress on thy cheeks.
My heart hath melted at a lady's tears,
Being an ordinary inundation,
But this effusion of such manly drops,

50 This shower, blown up by tempest of the soul,
Startles mine eyes, and makes me more amazed
Than had I seen the vaulty top of heaven
Figured quite o'er with burning meteors.
Lift up thy brow, renownèd Salisbury,

55 And with a great heart heave away this storm.
Commend these waters to those baby eyes
That never saw the giant world enraged,
Nor met with fortune other than at feasts,
Full warm of blood, of mirth, of gossiping.

60 Come, come; for thou shalt thrust thy hand as deep
Into the purse of rich prosperity
As Lewis himself. So, nobles, shall you all,
That knit your sinews to the strength of mine.

38 *vein* (1) blood vessel (2) mood   40 *temper* state of mind   41 *affections* emotions   44 *compulsion* what you were forced to do   *brave respect* courageous consideration of your true duty   45 *dew* i.e. tears   46 *progress* move slowly (like a king or queen in state; the metaphor emphasizes the nobility of Salisbury's tears)   53 *Figured* decorated   56 *Commend* leave   59 *Full . . . blood* full of human feeling

112

Enter Pandulph.

And even there, methinks, an angel spake.
Look, where the holy legate comes apace, 65
To give us warrant from the hand of heaven,
And on our actions set the name of right
With holy breath.
Pandulph.　　　　Hail, noble prince of France!
The next is this: King John hath reconciled
Himself to Rome; his spirit is come in 70
That so stood out against the holy church,
The great metropolis and see of Rome.
Therefore thy threat'ning colors now wind up,
And tame the savage spirit of wild war,
That, like a lion fostered up at hand, 75
It may lie gently at the foot of peace,
And be no further harmful than in show.
Lewis. Your grace shall pardon me; I will not back.
I am too high-born to be propertied,
To be a secondary at control, 80
Or useful serving-man and instrument
To any sovereign state throughout the world.
Your breath first kindled the dead coal of wars
Between this chastised kingdom and myself,
And brought in matter that should feed this fire; 85
And now 'tis far too huge to be blown out

64 *an angel spake* (has been variously explained: (1) a trumpet, like that of the angel announcing the last judgment, has just sounded (2) Pandulph, the angel since he bears heaven's warrant, has just entered (3) a pun on angel, a coin, with contemptuous reference to the Dauphin's mercenary motives) 67 *set* i.e. like a seal upon a warrant 70 *is come in* has submitted 78 *shall* must *back* retreat 79 *propertied* treated like property, made a tool of 80 *secondary at control* agent controlled by another 85 *matter* fuel

With that same weak wind which enkindled it.
You taught me how to know the face of right,
Acquainted me with interest to this land,
90   Yea, thrust this enterprise into my heart;
And come ye now to tell me John hath made
His peace with Rome? What is that peace to me?
I, by the honor of my marriage-bed,
After young Arthur, claim this land for mine,
95   And, now it is half-conquered, must I back
Because that John hath made his peace with Rome?
Am I Rome's slave? What penny hath Rome borne,
What men provided, what munition sent,
To underprop this action? Is 't not I
100   That undergo this charge? Who else but I,
And such as to my claim are liable,
Sweat in this business and maintain this war?
Have I not heard these islanders shout out,
Vive le roi! as I have banked their towns?
105   Have I not here the best cards for the game
To win this easy match played for a crown?
And shall I now give o'er the yielded set?
No, no, on my soul, it never shall be said.
Pandulph. You look but on the outside of this work.
110 *Lewis.* Outside or inside, I will not return
Till my attempt so much be glorified
As to my ample hope was promisèd
Before I drew this gallant head of war,
And culled these fiery spirits from the world,
115   To outlook conquest and to win renown

---

89 *interest to* claim in   99 *underprop* support   100 *charge* expense   101 *liable* subject   104 *banked* sailed by   107 *give o'er* abandon   *yielded set* game already forfeited to me   113 *head* army   114 *culled* carefully selected   115 *outlook* stare down

Even in the jaws of danger and of death.

                                        [Trumpet sounds.]

What lusty trumpet thus doth summon us?

                            Enter Bastard.

Bastard. According to the fair play of the world,
  Let me have audience; I am sent to speak.
  My holy Lord of Milan, from the king   120
  I come, to learn how you have dealt for him,
  And, as you answer, I do know the scope
  And warrant limited unto my tongue.
Pandulph. The Dauphin is too wilful-opposite,
  And will not temporize with my entreaties.   125
  He flatly says he'll not lay down his arms.
Bastard. By all the blood that ever fury breathed,
  The youth says well. Now hear our English king,
  For thus his royalty doth speak in me.
  He is prepared, and reason too he should.   130
  This apish and unmannerly approach,
  This harnessed masque and unadvisèd revel,
  This unhaired sauciness and boyish troops,
  The king doth smile at, and is well prepared
  To whip this dwarfish war, these pigmy arms,   135
  From out the circle of his territories.
  That hand which had the strength, even at your door,
  To cudgel you and make you take the hatch,
  To dive, like buckets, in concealèd wells,

117 *lusty* vigorous 118 *fair play* rules of chivalry 119 *to speak* i.e.
rather than to fight 122 *as* according as *scope* latitude 123 *limited*
appointed 124 *wilful-opposite* stubbornly hostile 125 *temporize* come
to terms 131 *apish* fantastic 132 *harnessed* in armor *unadvisèd revel*
thoughtless entertainment 133 *unhaired* beardless 136 *circle* compass
138 *take the hatch* leap over a half door or stile (like beaten dogs fleeing
their masters)

140   To crouch in litter of your stable planks,
         To lie like pawns locked up in chests and trunks,
         To hug with swine, to seek sweet safety out
         In vaults and prisons, and to thrill and shake
         Even at the crying of your nation's crow,
145   Thinking this voice an armèd Englishman —
         Shall that victorious hand be feebled here
         That in your chambers gave you chastisement?
         No! Know the gallant monarch is in arms,
         And like an eagle o'er his aery towers,
150   To souse annoyance that comes near his nest.
         And you degenerate, you ingrate revolts,
         You bloody Neroes, ripping up the womb
         Of your dear mother England, blush for shame;
         For your own ladies and pale-visaged maids
155   Like Amazons come tripping after drums,
         Their thimbles into armèd gauntlets change,
         Their needles to lances, and their gentle hearts
         To fierce and bloody inclination.
Lewis. There end thy brave, and turn thy face in peace.
160   We grant thou canst outscold us. Fare thee well.
         We hold our time too precious to be spent
         With such a brabbler.
Pandulph.   Give me leave to speak.
Bastard. No, I will speak.

---

140 *litter* bedding (for animals) *planks* floors   141 *pawns* articles in pawn
144 *your nation's crow* sound of the rooster, traditional symbol of France
149 *aery* eagle's nest   *towers* soars   150 *souse* swoop down on (like a bird
of prey)   *annoyance* threat of danger   151 *ingrate revolts* ungrateful rebels
152 *Neroes* (the Roman emperor Nero was said to have ripped open his
mother's womb after murdering her)   155 *Amazons* female warriors of
Greek mythology   157 *needles* (monosyllable; in folio, 'Needl's')   158 *in-
clination* (1) disposition (2) the slanting position of a knight charging with a
lance (a quibble)   159 *brave* defiant boast   162 *brabbler* braggart

Lewis.   We will attend to neither.
　Strike up the drums, and let the tongue of war
　Plead for our interest and our being here.   **165**
Bastard. Indeed, your drums, being beaten, will cry out,
　And so shall you, being beaten. Do but start
　An echo with the clamor of thy drum,
　And even at hand a drum is ready braced
　That shall reverberate all as loud as thine.   **170**
　Sound but another, and another shall
　As loud as thine rattle the welkin's ear
　And mock the deep-mouthed thunder. For at hand —
　Not trusting to this halting legate here,
　Whom he hath used rather for sport than need —   **175**
　Is warlike John; and in his forehead sits
　A bare-ribbed death, whose office is this day
　To feast upon whole thousands of the French.
Lewis. Strike up our drums to find this danger out.
Bastard. And thou shalt find it, Dauphin, do not doubt.   **180**
　　　　　　　　　　　　　　　　Exeunt.

Alarums. Enter [King] John and Hubert.   **V, iii**

King John. How goes the day with us? O, tell me, Hubert.
Hubert. Badly, I fear. How fares your majesty?
King John. This fever that hath troubled me so long
　Lies heavy on me. O, my heart is sick!

163 *attend* listen 169 *braced* with tightened skin, ready for playing 172
welkin's sky's 174 *halting* wavering, ineffectual 177 *bare-ribbed death*
i.e. death conceived of as a skeleton *office* function

Enter a Messenger.

5 *Messenger.* My lord, your valiant kinsman, Faulconbridge,
   Desires your majesty to leave the field
   And send him word by me which way you go.
   King John. Tell him, toward Swinstead, to the abbey there.
   Messenger. Be of good comfort, for the great supply
10   That was expected by the Dauphin here,
   Are wracked three nights ago on Goodwin sands.
   This news was brought to Richard but even now.
   The French fight coldly and retire themselves.
   King John. Ay me! This tyrant fever burns me up,
15   And will not let me welcome this good news.
   Set on toward Swinstead. To my litter straight;
   Weakness possesseth me, and I am faint.   *Exeunt.*

V, iv   *Enter Salisbury, Pembroke, and Bigot.*

   Salisbury. I did not think the king so stored with friends.
   Pembroke. Up once again; put spirit in the French.
   If they miscarry we miscarry too.
   Salisbury. That misbegotten devil, Faulconbridge,
5   In spite of spite, alone upholds the day.
   Pembroke. They say King John, sore sick, hath left the field.

Enter Melun wounded.

   Melun. Lead me to the revolts of England here.
   Salisbury. When we were happy we had other names.

V, iii, 9 *supply* reinforcements   11 *wracked* shipwrecked   13 *coldly* without enthusiasm   14 *tyrant* merciless   V, iv, 1 *stored* provided   5 *In spite
of spite* despite anything we can do   7 *revolts* rebels

Pembroke. It is the Count Melun.

Salisbury.   Wounded to death.

Melun. Fly, noble English; you are bought and sold.   10
    Unthread the rude eye of rebellion,
    And welcome home again discarded faith.
    Seek out King John and fall before his feet,
    For if the French be lords of this loud day,
    He means to recompense the pains you take   15
    By cutting off your heads. Thus hath he sworn,
    And I with him, and many moe with me,
    Upon the altar at Saint Edmundsbury,
    Even on that altar where we swore to you
    Dear amity and everlasting love.   20

Salisbury. May this be possible? May this be true?

Melun. Have I not hideous death within my view,
    Retaining but a quantity of life,
    Which bleeds away, even as a form of wax
    Resolveth from his figure 'gainst the fire?   25
    What in the world should make me now deceive,
    Since I must lose the use of all deceit?
    Why should I then be false, since it is true
    That I must die here and live hence by truth?
    I say again, if Lewis do win the day,   30
    He is forsworn if e'er those eyes of yours
    Behold another day break in the east.
    But even this night, whose black contagious breath

10 *bought and sold* betrayed 11 *Unthread . . . eye* retrace your steps (as
a thread is withdrawn from the needle's eye) 15 *He* i.e. the Dauphin
17 *moe* more 23 *quantity* small amount 24–25 *as a form . . . fire* (witches
were said to destroy their enemies by melting waxen images of them before
a fire) 25 *Resolveth* dissolves *his figure* its shape 27 *use* profit, advantage 29 *live hence by truth* i.e. he will live in heaven to the extent that he
has been truthful on earth 31 *forsworn* perjured 33 *contagious* bearing
disease

Already smokes about the burning crest
35 Of the old, feeble, and day-wearied sun,
Even this ill night, your breathing shall expire,
Paying the fine of rated treachery
Even with a treacherous fine of all your lives,
If Lewis by your assistance win the day.
40 Commend me to one Hubert with your king.
The love of him, and this respect besides,
For that my grandsire was an Englishman,
Awakes my conscience to confess all this.
In lieu whereof, I pray you, bear me hence
45 From forth the noise and rumor of the field,
Where I may think the remnant of my thoughts
In peace, and part this body and my soul
With contemplation and devout desires.
Salisbury. We do believe thee, and beshrew my
soul
50 But I do love the favor and the form
Of this most fair occasion, by the which
We will untread the steps of damnèd flight,
And like a bated and retirèd flood,
Leaving our rankness and irregular course,
55 Stoop low within those bounds we have o'erlooked,
And calmly run on in obedience
Even to our ocean, to our great King John.
My arm shall give thee help to bear thee hence,
For I do see the cruel pangs of death

---

34 *smokes* grows misty (as evening approaches)   37 *fine* penalty   *rated*
(1) exposed at its true value (2) rebuked, punished   38 *fine* end (note
quibble)   41 *respect* consideration   42 *For that* because   44 *In lieu where-*
of in payment for which   45 *rumor* noise   49 *beshrew* a curse upon   50 *favor*
and the form outward appearance   52 *untread* retrace   53 *bated* abated
54 *rankness* overgrowth   55 *o'erlooked* overflowed

Right in thine eye. Away, my friends! New flight,   60
And happy newness, that intends old right.
                        Exeunt [leading off Melun].

                Enter [Lewis, the] Dauphin, and his train.   V, v

Lewis. The sun of heaven methought was loath to set,
But stayed and made the western welkin blush,
When English measure backward their own ground
In faint retire. O, bravely came we off,
When with a volley of our needless shot,   5
After such bloody toil, we bid good night
And wound our tott'ring colors clearly up,
Last in the field, and almost lords of it!

                Enter a Messenger.

Messenger. Where is my prince, the Dauphin?
Lewis.   Here. What news?
Messenger. The Count Melun is slain. The English lords,   10
By his persuasion, are again fall'n off,
And your supply, which you have wished so long,
Are cast away and sunk on Goodwin sands.
Lewis. Ah, foul, shrewd news! Beshrew thy very heart!
I did not think to be so sad to-night   15

60 *Right* clearly   61 *happy newness* propitious change   V, v, 2 *welkin* sky
4 *faint retire* timid retreat   *bravely* excellently   *came we off* we retired
from battle   7 *tott'ring* (1) wavering (2) in tatters (rags)   *colors* banners
clearly neatly, without interference from the enemy   11 *are again fall'n
off* have again broken faith   12 *supply* reinforcements   14 *shrewd* grievous,
bitter   *Beshrew* curse

As this hath made me. Who was he that said
King John did fly an hour or two before
The stumbling night did part our weary powers?
Messenger. Whoever spoke it, it is true, my lord.
20 *Lewis.* Well, keep good quarter and good care to-night.
The day shall not be up so soon as I
To try the fair adventure of to-morrow.   *Exeunt*

V, vi   *Enter Bastard and Hubert, severally.*

Hubert. Who's there? Speak, ho! Speak quickly, or I shoot.
Bastard. A friend. What art thou?
Hubert.   Of the part of England.
Bastard. Whither dost thou go?
Hubert. What's that to thee? Why may not I demand
5 Of thine affairs as well as thou of mine?
Bastard. Hubert, I think?
Hubert.   Thou hast a perfect thought.
I will upon all hazards well believe
Thou art my friend, that know'st my tongue so well.
Who art thou?
Bastard.   Who thou wilt; and if thou please,
10 Thou mayst befriend me so much as to think
I come one way of the Plantagenets.
Hubert. Unkind remembrance! Thou and eyeless night
Have done me shame. Brave soldier, pardon me,

---

18 *stumbling* causing to stumble   20 *quarter* watch   22 *fair adventure* good
fortune   V, vi, 2 *Of the part* on the side   6 *perfect* correct   12 *remembrance*
memory   *eyeless* i.e. black   13 *done me shame* disgraced me (by causing
my discourteous failure to recognize a friend)

That any accent breaking from thy tongue
Should scape the true acquaintance of mine ear.   15
Bastard. Come, come! Sans compliment, what news
    abroad?
Hubert. Why, here walk I in the black brow of night
To find you out.
Bastard.   Brief, then; and what's the news?
Hubert. O, my sweet sir, news fitting to the night,
Black, fearful, comfortless, and horrible.   20
Bastard. Show me the very wound of this ill news.
I am no woman; I'll not swound at it.
Hubert. The king, I fear, is poisoned by a monk.
I left him almost speechless and broke out
To acquaint you with this evil, that you might   25
The better arm you to the sudden time
Than if you had at leisure known of this.
Bastard. How did he take it? Who did taste to him?
Hubert. A monk, I tell you, a resolvèd villain,
Whose bowels suddenly burst out. The king   30
Yet speaks and peradventure may recover.
Bastard. Whom didst thou leave to tend his majesty?
Hubert. Why, know you not? The lords are all come back,
And brought Prince Henry in their company,
At whose request the king hath pardoned them,   35
And they are all about his majesty.
Bastard. Withhold thine indignation, mighty heaven,
And tempt us not to bear above our power!
I'll tell thee, Hubert, half my power this night,

14 *accent* speech 16 *Sans compliment* without formal speech 22 *swound*
faint 24 *broke out* rushed away 26 *arm . . . time* prepare yourself for
the emergency 27 *at leisure* after delay 28 *taste to* serve as food
taster for 29 *resolvèd* determined 31 *peradventure* perhaps 38 *tempt*
. . power do not test us by making us endure more than we are able to
39 *power* army

123

40 Passing these flats, are taken by the tide.
    These Lincoln Washes have devourèd them.
    Myself, well mounted, hardly have escaped.
    Away before! Conduct me to the king;
    I doubt he will be dead or ere I come.   *Exeunt*

V, vii   *Enter Prince Henry, Salisbury, and Bigot.*

  Prince Henry. It is too late. The life of all his blood
    Is touched corruptibly, and his pure brain,
    Which some suppose the soul's frail dwelling-house,
    Doth, by the idle comments that it makes,
5   Foretell the ending of mortality.

                 Enter Pembroke.

  Pembroke. His highness yet doth speak, and holds belief
    That, being brought into the open air,
    It would allay the burning quality
    Of that fell poison which assaileth him.
10 *Prince Henry.* Let him be brought into the orchard here.
    Doth he still rage?   *[Exit Bigot.*
  Pembroke.   He is more patient
    Than when you left him; even now he sung.
  Prince Henry. O, vanity of sickness! Fierce extremes
    In their continuance will not feel themselves.
15 Death, having preyed upon the outward parts,
    Leaves them invisible, and his siege is now

40 *flats* low lands near the sea 42 *hardly* barely 44 *doubt* fear V, vii, 2
touched corruptibly infected so as to cause corruption 4 *idle* foolish 5 *mor-*
tality life 6 *yet* still 9 *fell* cruel 11 *rage* rave 13 *extremes* extremitie
14 *In . . . themselves* as they continue cease to be felt 16 *invisible* (modi
fies 'Death')

Against the mind, the which he pricks and wounds
With many legions of strange fantasies,
Which, in their throng and press to that last hold,
Confound themselves. 'Tis strange that death should sing. 20
I am the cygnet to this pale faint swan,
Who chants a doleful hymn to his own death,
And from the organ-pipe of frailty sings
His soul and body to their lasting rest.
..lisbury. Be of good comfort, prince, for you are born   25
To set a form upon that indigest
Which he hath left so shapeless and so rude.

[King] John brought in.

..ing John. Ay, marry, now my soul hath elbow-room.
It would not out at windows, nor at doors.
There is so hot a summer in my bosom   30
That all my bowels crumble up to dust.
I am a scribbled form, drawn with a pen
Upon a parchment, and against this fire
Do I shrink up.
..ince Henry.   How fares your majesty?
..ing John. Poisoned — ill fare! Dead, forsook, cast off, 35
And none of you will bid the winter come
To thrust his icy fingers in my maw,
Nor let my kingdom's rivers take their course
Through my burned bosom, nor entreat the north
To make his bleak winds kiss my parchèd lips   40
And comfort me with cold. I do not ask you much.

fantasies hallucinations 19 *throng and press* disordered rush *hold*
..onghold (the mind) 20 *Confound themselves* destroy one another (i.e. his
..lirious thoughts negate one another so that he is totally incoherent)
..cygnet young swan (the swan was said to sing only one song during his
..e, just before his death) 26 *indigest* shapeless mass, state of confu-
..n 35 *ill fare* (1) ill lot (2) bad food 37 *maw* throat

I beg cold comfort; and you are so strait
And so ingrateful, you deny me that.
Prince Henry. O, that there were some virtue in my tears
That might relieve you.
45 *King John.*   The salt in them is hot.
Within me is a hell, and there the poison
Is as a fiend confined to tyrannize
On unreprievable condemnèd blood.

Enter Bastard.

Bastard. O, I am scalded with my violent motion
50   And spleen of speed to see your majesty.
King John. O cousin, thou art come to set mine eye!
The tackle of my heart is cracked and burnt,
And all the shrouds wherewith my life should sail
Are turnèd to one thread, one little hair.
55   My heart hath one poor string to stay it by,
Which holds but till thy news be utterèd,
And then all this thou seest is but a clod
And module of confounded royalty.
Bastard. The Dauphin is preparing hitherward,
60   Where heaven he knows how we shall answer him,
For in a night the best part of my power,
As I upon advantage did remove,
Were in the Washes all unwarily
Devourèd by the unexpected flood.   *[The King dies.]*

42 *strait* niggardly   44 *virtue* healing power   48 *unreprievable* beyond re-
prieve   49 *scalded* heated   50 *spleen* eagerness   51 *set mine eyes* i.e. close
my eyes in death   52 *tackle* rigging of a ship   53 *shrouds* ropes supporting
the mast of a ship   58 *module* mere image   *confounded* destroyed   60 *heaven*
he knows only God knows   62 *upon advantage* to take advantage of a favorable opportunity   *remove* change position   63 *unwarily* unexpectedly
64 *unexpected flood* sudden flowing in of the tide

Salisbury. You breathe these dead news in as dead an ear.   65
    My liege! My lord! But now a king, now thus!
Prince Henry. Even so must I run on, and even so stop.
    What surety of the world, what hope, what stay,
    When this was now a king, and now is clay?
Bastard. Art thou gone so? I do but stay behind   70
    To do the office for thee of revenge,
    And then my soul shall wait on thee to heaven,
    As it on earth hath been thy servant still.
    Now, now, you stars that move in your right spheres,
    Where be your powers? Show now your mended faiths,   75
    And instantly return with me again,
    To push destruction and perpetual shame
    Out of the weak door of our fainting land.
    Straight let us seek, or straight we shall be sought.
    The Dauphin rages at our very heels.   80
Salisbury. It seems you know not, then, so much as we.
    The Cardinal Pandulph is within at rest,
    Who half an hour since came from the Dauphin,
    And brings from him such offers of our peace
    As we with honor and respect may take,   85
    With purpose presently to leave this war.
Bastard. He will the rather do it when he sees
    Ourselves well sinewèd to our defense.
Salisbury. Nay, 'tis in a manner done already;
    For many carriages he hath dispatched   90
    To the seaside, and put his cause and quarrel
    To the disposing of the cardinal;

65 *dead news* (1) deadly news (2) news of death   68 *surety* certainty   *stay* support   73 *still* always   74 *stars . . . spheres* i.e. noblemen who have returned to their proper allegiance (revolving around the throne, as stars were believed in a harmonious cosmos to revolve around the earth)   75 *powers* armies   *mended faiths* restored loyalties   79 *Straight* immediately   85 *respect* self-respect   88 *sinewèd* strengthened   90 *carriages* vehicles

With whom yourself, myself, and other lords,
If you think meet, this afternoon will post
95 To consummate this business happily.

Bastard. Let it be so. And you, my noble prince,
With other princes that may best be spared,
Shall wait upon your father's funeral.

Prince Henry. At Worcester must his body be interred,
For so he willed it.

100 *Bastard.*   Thither shall it then.
And happily may your sweet self put on
The lineal state and glory of the land!
To whom, with all submission, on my knee,
I do bequeath my faithful services
105 And true subjection everlastingly.

Salisbury. And the like tender of our love we make,
To rest without a spot for evermore.

Prince Henry. I have a kind soul that would give you
    thanks,
And knows not how to do it but with tears.

110 *Bastard.* O, let us pay the time but needful woe,
Since it hath been beforehand with our griefs.
This England never did, nor never shall,
Lie at the proud foot of a conqueror
But when it first did help to wound itself.
115 Now these her princes are come home again,
Come the three corners of the world in arms,
And we shall shock them. Nought shall make us rue
If England to itself do rest but true.   *Exeunt.*

---

101 *happily* propitiously   102 *lineal state* kingship by right of birth   106
tender offer   107 *spot* blemish (of disloyalty)   110–11 *let . . . griefs* i.e. let
us not weep more than necessary, since we have already paid the sad occasion enough of the grief due to it   116 *three corners* i.e. the rest of the
world, England being the fourth corner   117 *shock* meet them with force